This book is dedicated to the adventurous world-changers and multi-creative leaders who desire to create a greater future, together.

Know that every choice to create, creates.

Is it time to stop hiding your brilliance?

STOP WAITING, START CREATING

LISA MURRAY

National Library of Australia Cataloguing-In-Publication data:

Title: STOP WAITING, START CREATING
Author: Murray, Lisa
ISBN 978-0-9942433-1-7
Subjects: creativity, business, procrastination, mindset, self-help

COPYRIGHT © 2016 by Lisa Murray and Enriched Publishing
The moral rights of the author have been asserted.

All rights reserved. Except as permitted under the Australian Copyright Act 1968, no part of this book may be used or reproduced by any means graphic, electronic or mechanical, stored in a retrieval system, communicated, copied or transmitted in any form or by any means including photocopying, recording or taping without prior written permission.

Editor: Cassandra Russell
Cover Illustration & Design: Shayna Fernando
Internal Layout & Design: Heather Bell
Photographer: My Södergren

First published in 2016 by Enriched Enterprises Pty Ltd
PO Box 77, Tewantin QLD 4565 Australia

DISCLAIMER: This book is not intended to provide personalised legal, financial or investment advice. The authors and the publisher specifically disclaim any liability, loss or risk which is incurred as a consequence, directly or indirectly through the use and application of any contents of this work. Any websites referenced in this book may change without notice.

www.CreativityLab.tv
www.BusinessAlchemyLab.com
lisa@creativitylab.tv

BONUS RESOURCES: **www.CreativityLab.tv/SWSC**

TABLE OF CONTENTS

INTRODUCTION 13

WHAT IF... YOU ARE AN UNSTOPPABLE CREATOR? 13

~SECTION 1~ 15

IS NOW YOUR TIME? 15

IGNITING THE DESIRE TO CREATE 17
   Beyond The Inertia Epidemic 21
   Why Create? 23

DON'T START WITH WHY! 25
   How Do You Know You Are Different? 26
   Start Where You Are 28
   Where Are Your Creative Energies Hiding? 29
   What If It's Time To Change
   The Status Quo? 30
   'But It's Easy For You...' 34
   What Is Creation? 36
   Not My Circus, Not My Monkeys! 39

WHAT IF... YOU'RE NOT WRONG? 41
   Positive Judgment Is Still Judgement 45

WHAT'S STOPPING YOU? 51
   "But I'm Not Creative" 53
   "I Haven't Got Time" 55
   "I've Lost My Creative Edge" 58
   "I'm Waiting..." 59
   "No-one Is Interested In What I Have To Offer" 63

"I Don't Know Enough to Start - I'm a Fraud!" 69
"I'm Scared of Being Visible" 72
"I Won't…" 75
"I Don't Know Where To Start" 77
"I'm So Distracted!" 79
Being TOO Much! The Myth That Keeps You Small 82
"I Don't Have The Perfect Plan… Yet!" 84
"I'm Too Tired To Be Creative" 86
"My 'To-Do' List is Way Too Long!" 88
What Makes You Limit Yourself? 90

OUT-CREATING YOUR CREATIVE BLOCKS *95*
When Creating Is Too Slow or Too Boring 96
Are You Willing To Be BAD? 97
The Adventure of Being Out-Of-Control 99
What If Your Idea Isn't Working? 101

5 ELEMENTS OF CREATING *103*
Spontaneity 104
Flexibility 111
Exploration & Curiosity 114
Flow 122
Creativity 125
Tenacity {Surprise! There's a Sixth Element!} 127

~SECTION 2~ **133**

WHAT ARE YOU CREATING? **133**

CREATIVE CLARITY: CHOOSING WHAT TO CREATE *135*
The 'What To Create?' Question 137
Start With Your Brilliance, Not Your Passion 138
Let's Get Specific. What Are You Going To Create? 142
A Creative Project? 144
Are You Creating A Business? 146
Are You Creating Your Life? 149

How Do You Start?.... YOU. JUST. START!..........................151
Your First Priority Is To START!..152
Refuse To Do It 'Right' 156
Start Being Creative In Every Detail Of Your Life..............158

PURPOSE, PASSION, PROFIT... OR PLAY? *161*
Your Passion...162
Your Purpose 163
Play… It's Not Just For Kids! 167
Loving Your Creations..169

CREATION, DESTRUCTION & CHANGE....................................*173*
Creating From Destruction 175
What Are You Asking To Create?..177
Creating By Request 179

CREATING ISN'T LOGICAL...*181*
Questions Create. Conclusions Contract! 183
Creating From The Past..185
Right Timing 186
Following Your Inspiration..188

~SECTION 3~ **191**

EXPLORING YOUR CREATIVE PROCESS **191**

NURTURING YOUR CREATIVE PROCESSES..........................*193*
Identifying Your Creative Process 197
Discovering You Are Creative 200

MULTIPLE PROJECTS – THE NEW MULTI-TASKING............*203*
Not Enough Ideas (Or No Ideas!) 205
Overwhelm 207
Too Many Ideas - No Idea Where To Start? 211
Nothing Ever Gets Completed...212
Simplify to Amplify 215

Are Your Ideas BIG Enough?..218
Is Having Multiple Projects Still Freaking You Out? 219

DOING & FIXING IS NOT CREATING..*221*
   BEing or DOing? 222
   Fixing Shit Is Overrated 226

CREATING FROM (THE BLANK) SPACE....................................*231*
   Creating In The Unknown 233
   The Most Under-rated Creation Tool Ever! 236
   Inviting The Whispers of the Future 238
   What if Focus Is a Limitation?...239
   Work Less. Create More! 241
   Hanging Out In Nature...243
   Creating In The Wee Hours 244

CONNECTION, COLLABORATION &
CO-CREATION *247*
   Connections 249
   Collaborations & Co-Creations 254

THE HEDONISM OF FINISHING..*259*
   The Adventure of Finishing...261
   Are Your Projects Shouting 'Finish ME!'? 264
   Stop Your Unfinished Projects From Distracting You........266
   Making Finishing FUN! 269
   What If Finishing Doesn't Have a Happy Ending? 273

~SECTION 4~ 275

CREATING BEYOND WHAT EXISTS! 275

WHAT KIND OF WORLD WOULD YOU CREATE? *277*
   Controversy, Rebellion & Leadership 277
   Rebellion Is Not The Answer 279

~SECTION 5~ 289

WHAT'S NEXT? 289

CONNECT WITH LISA MURRAY & CREATIVITY LAB 291
Creativity Lab – Online Programs 292
Creativity Lab - Live Events 292
Private Coaching With Lisa Murray 293
Connect With Lisa Online 293

INTRODUCTION

WHAT IF... YOU ARE AN UNSTOPPABLE CREATOR?

This is a book about creating your beautiful ideas, not living in a constant state of fixing problems. Have you noticed that people spend most of their time and money on fixing their life rather than having the pleasure of living? They spend every waking hour solving problems. It's time for a new dominant paradigm on the planet. Creation not Fix-ation! If you are going to fix everything before you begin creating, you'll never start.

If you love creating shit to fix and you don't want to create anything new in the world, please don't buy this book. If you love creating, and there's a few temporary obstacles stopping you, this book has been created especially for you!

My desire is for every person on planet earth to be able to create the life and the reality they desire. Not from a space of what's not working, but from a space of what's possible. This book is an invitation to a new way of being in the world. To a new way of creating your ideas, your life and your desires. Imagine living in a world where what you desire to create is more relevant and desirable than focusing on the problems you think you have to fix.

The tools you need to get over your obstacles are inside the book. Even more useful, there is a system for discovering your personal capacities with creating. You may find this book uncomfortable in places, or even confronting and my suggestion is to keep reading! The wondrous thing about creating is, if you embrace the possibilities rather than what you are not (yet) creating, you'll keep moving forward.

To create is to bring into being from nothing, to make or form, to produce, to generate and to form anew. The dictionary does not mention 'to fix'. It's time to expand your capacity to out-create what exists. If you were the leader of the entire world, what would you create? The good news is - You are the leader in your world. Let's start!

Lisa Murray
Creation Catalyst, Creativity Lab
www.CreativityLab.tv
www.BusinessAlchemyLab.com

~SECTION 1~
IS NOW YOUR TIME?

IGNITING THE DESIRE TO CREATE

Moments of creative transformation come not by thinking, but by being willing to receive the creative genius that is who we truly are. Creating comes with play, joy, magic, adventure, spontaneity and dynamic 'aha' moments. It comes quiet, soft and sweet, weaving its way into your world, as you allow it the space to evolve. It comes with confidence, conscious awareness, collaboration, and sometimes confusion! It comes with knowing the unknown, and becoming present with the intangible. It comes intuitively, with a wordless clarity that can be interpreted in many subtle ways.

Creating is the essence of physically expressing you on planet earth. It's the energy of what you do and be in every moment, whether you acknowledge this or not. Every single thing in your world was created… by you, by your choices, by your engagement with everything and everyone around you.

If you'd like any part of your life or your world to be different, you start by creating and generating new

Lisa Murray

possibilities. Whether you are reading this book because what you have is not enough, or you are secretly tired of languishing in the false sense of security that is your comfort bubble, or you just know there has to be more enjoyable ways of creating your dreams and desires, this book offers a plethora of ideas, tools and techniques, for creating the difference you are asking for.

Do you recall your capacity for creation as a child? Did you ever go without what you truly desired? Or did you always find a way forward? Did you embrace the magic of this planet and beyond, until you were ridiculed for your fantasies and fairy friends? Or did you delight in getting your hands dirty, in creating with whatever materials found their way to you? Did you engage in the creation of other worlds through video games? Did you read books to immerse yourself in stories more exciting than your life? All of this was your desire for creation, bursting out of you in whatever way it could.

If this wasn't your childhood, it's not too late to have something even more wonderful. Even if your desire to create was squashed out of you with your very first breath, you can invite your creative energies to play in any moment. Our history of creating can only include limitations if we allow that to be so. The story is just the story. Right now you have choice to create! You can create the 'same same' you've always had... or the 'same same but one degree different'... or you can expand your possible futures by inviting your unique differences to show up in every moment. You get to choose! Today! Now!

I am grateful for growing up in playful environments where I was encouraged to create new adventures every day. Grateful that my parents made us create the money

STOP WAITING, START CREATING

for everything we wanted, even from a young age (and even if it wasn't so much fun at the time!). Grateful that I learned there is always another way forward, even if I don't know what it is yet.

If you consider the creative environment you grew up in, there were always choices, always possibilities, always a different question you could ask. And yet, somewhere along life's journey, we stop those energies, instead putting our attention to what limits us, what paralyses us, what blocks us... buying the lie that we can't create, that we don't have what it takes and that we don't know how.

Even with my wildly creative childhood, there have been times I've embraced these kinds of lies as if they were real and true for me. No. They were the ways I allowed me to stop me. The ways I allowed me to be small, insignificant and impotent. The ways I hid my brilliance. The ways I pretended to be less than I am.

When I made the demand for all of that to change, my life once again became a generative, playful moment by moment adventure. It is this sense of wonder and delight that I invite you to in "Stop Waiting, Start Creating".

Every environment is creative because we are creative. When I lived with someone who was abusive, my creative capacities showed up in different ways to how they are when I'm living in happy spaces. Your environment does not stop you. You stop you. And that's what this book invites you to change!

It's not always easy to admit that we stop ourselves. We like to think it's because of something or someone else, and that can only be true when we've given our creative capacities away in favour of making someone else happy. When we move beyond the desire to stop ourselves from creating, literally anything and everything becomes possible.

Every day amazing possibilities show up in my world that were not part of my reality when I was allowing others to determine my creative choices. Bliss shows up when we show up. Bliss shows up when our presence becomes greater than the distractions we allow ourselves to inhabit as if they are real. We can create like dinosaurs responded to change (and you know what happened to them!), or we can create with the nimbleness and acuity of a bee.

What would be different if you would create like a bee? Never allowing anything to distract you from pollinating the blooming blossoms that your creations can become. Making it possible for this planet to thrive with your ideas. Bringing your specific gifts into the world in ways that only you can. Nurturing yourself so that you can continue to produce the flavoursome creations that you do. Knowing exactly which flower to create with next, and knowing when to move on. Changing the world, with the tiniest flap of your amazing wings. Being the magic that shows others how the impossibility of flying is simply a myth you buy until the moment you set yourself free. If a bee can fly beyond its physical limits, so can you!

You might have already noticed this book is different. I am different. I mostly use both left and right brains which creates some very different perspectives. Sometimes people look at me oddly because my brain has a gift for extrapolation. I see connections and ideas where others do not! Maybe you have a different way of creating too! Are you ready to embrace all of your creative capacities? Even the ones other people make wrong?

STOP WAITING, START CREATING

For a long time I tried to create like other people think is 'right' i.e. logical and orderly and linearly. It didn't really work for me and as soon as I started my businesses, I reverted to creating my way! Each of us has different ways of creating. There isn't one 'right' way. There is just your way.

Throughout this book you need to ask questions like 'Is this relevant to me?' and 'How do I do this different?' and 'What is MY way of creating this?' And as we go forward, you'll probably enjoy a few reminders of ways you love to create, that you've given up because of someone else's point of view! Most of us stop creating because our ways of creating have been made wrong. When we stop, we paralyse ourselves, creating inertia and limiting what is truly possible.

To start exploring what your ways of creating are and what you know about your ways, download the free Creative Alchemy e-class which takes you on an adventure in trusting your intuitive knowing. www.CreativityLab.tv/Alchemy

Beyond The Inertia Epidemic

Have you noticed there's an inertia epidemic? The symptoms include boredom, anxiety, self-sabotage, procrastination, tiredness, fear, trying to make everything perfect, not having time... People are allowing themselves to be frozen by the immense changes going on in the world. It is stopping them from creating; stopping them from choosing a different future.

Lisa Murray

If you feel like everything has stopped, everything is stuck, everything (including you) is wrong, you need to get a sense of whether this is truly you, or whether you are just aware of the intensity of the unseen change that is going on underneath the surface. It is an amazing time to be alive! We are balanced on the tip of an iceberg that is about to break away from all that has been.

Underneath us, everything is shifting and changing. It's easy to sense the dis-ease, the un-ease and the overwhelming need to please and fit in. When we try to create safety, we are trying to refuse change. When we resist change we also stop the possibilities for greater futures.

When you become aware of the 'stop' energy that is permeating the world, you begin to realise that is a choice too. You can live like a limpet, stubbornly clinging to the closest rock even to the point of destruction; you can choose to live like a lemming, copying everyone around you; ...or you can allow your creative energies to emerge as a powerhouse full of new possibilities. What are you going to choose? Limpet? Lemming? or YOU?

Whatever inertia symptoms you are experiencing, the first question to ask is "Is this mine? Or am I just highly aware of what's changing on planet earth and with the people around me?" If you know when an angry person enters a room, even before they speak, chances are you are aware of all the people suffering and stagnating their way through the inertia epidemic. What if you don't have to join them?

Why Create?

Why create? It's a great question and in the next chapter, we will look at why 'WHY' is not the first question you need to ask! Simon Sinek made 'Start With Why' famous with his book of the same name. And starting with why won't work if you are still stuck in the inertia epidemic.

To start with why, you need to be willing to be inspired. To be inspired you need to move past what is creating your inertia. You need to let go of what stops you, so that you have the space to receive what inspires you.

After years of allowing all kinds of crazy things to stop me, I've come to a space where inertia is rarely present in my world. Doing the inner work has been a gift to me beyond words. When you play with the energies of creation, instead of the energies of inertia, everything in your life becomes more enjoyable! In Section One 'Is Now Your Time?' we're going to release the inertia and move towards what inspires you.

In Section Two 'What Are You Creating?' we're going to explore your 'why' and how to choose what to create. Once you remove the inertia, there are SO many choices! My personal 'why' comes from one question... "What would I like the world to be like 1,000 years from now?" It's a big part of what inspired me to write this book. I saw that people didn't have joy and ease with creating in the ways I know are possible.

Lisa Murray

A thousand years from now, (or way sooner!!!) I'd love people to be able to create whatever they desire, instantly and with ease. I'd love the world to be a kinder, more nurturing, more joyful place. I'd love every person to trust themselves... and to know that they can be what will create everything they desire. I'd love people to contribute to each other so that everyone can have more. Whatever I create, these are the energies I include. It's a fun way to play with living, leading and working.

In Section Three 'Exploring Your Creative Process' we play with your ways of creating. We talk about ways of creating that go way beyond what everyone says are the 'right' ways of creating. We go deeper into those situations where it is challenging to create and we explore what new models of creating can contribute to the choices we have available.

In Section Four 'Creating Beyond What Exists' we explore what kind of world you want to create and how you can make a difference to you and the Universe, in a way that you love.

This book is about igniting the desire to create, so that you can always have more of what makes you happy. When you are happy, you are being you. When you are being you, you are creating what is possible for you to create. Your purpose is always clear and always evolving. Your life becomes an intriguing adventure, instead of being filled with the sleepy inertia that you secretly know is not enough for you. Shall we play?

DON'T START WITH WHY!

"The sky is filled with stars, invisible by day." ~ **Henry Wadsworth Longfellow**

Did you ever look up at the night sky in wonder? Ever wish you were that bright and brilliant? What if you ARE the stars? Physics shows that virtually everything on earth, including us, is made of stardust. Yes… you are the stars! And you're slinking about in the daylight, hiding your talents and gifts from the world so that you won't be 'too different' or 'too amazing' or even 'too much'!

If you are that brilliant, you must have a purpose for living. And if you are like most people, you won't begin to create until you know what your purpose is. If you are running around wondering what to create and desperately seeking your purpose or your 'why', know this…

You can't start with your 'why' if you won't acknowledge your brilliance or your difference. You can have the biggest 'why' in the Universe and it will still taste like cardboard if you don't include your special sauce!

I hid my brilliance and my difference for a long time. At school I was teased and bullied for it. At university I was sometimes resented for it. In workplaces it was often only begrudgingly appreciated and also, actively undermined. So I unconsciously adopted a habit of hiding, which was a way of creating against myself and my desires so that other people would not be so uncomfortable around me.

A few years ago one of my mentors told me not to worry about getting on television because I didn't think I had anything to say. He was deliberately planting a seed to see if I would start to acknowledge who I truly am and how different and brilliant I am. I was a little slow off the starting blocks, but eventually I got it. His cheeky wisecrack worked!

How Do You Know You Are Different?

You ask 'Is this how everyone else does it?' or 'Is trying to do this like everyone else making me fail?' Once you are clear that you don't create like everyone else, you've got a place to start! I've always known I was different, but I didn't know why or how. I just knew that mostly I didn't fit in.

Most people start with the 'why' and get stuck there when they run into their personal limitations and excuses. Start with removing the excuses for not creating. The

STOP WAITING, START CREATING

'why' for most people changes as they remove their limitations!

Before I could discover my 'why' or create ideas big enough to hold my attention, I had to discover who I truly desired to BE. And who I truly am that I've been pretending I'm not! If you don't know WHO you are, your 'why' will flip-flop at the whim of any bright shiny new object whizzing by. I wonder if you have ever experienced this?

A few years ago my 'why' started off with a very big idea that had very little energy behind it. Someone had given me the words that carried an inviting future possibility, but I was not yet willing to BE the person who could create that. I had too many self-imposed limitations sitting on top of my brilliance! It really isn't fun to go through life with an elephant sitting on your head! Elephants are big and heavy and they break everything as they silently tramp through the jungle. When you embrace who you are more fully, that elephant can turn into a lion, roaring into life as the leader in your world.

I've stopped trying to define my 'why' in any kind of static fixed way. My 'why' expands and changes as I grow into being way more of me; as I release my limitations; as I become willing to choose beyond my comfort zone; as I keep discovering that what I desired just a few short years ago is nowhere near enough for me!

Growing up is not about getting older, it's about growing into the beauty and magic of who you truly are. Imagine what could be possible if you would stop resisting that? (And stop pretending that age has anything to do with anything…)

Every choice I've made to stop allowing my excuses to own me and stop me has resulted in a greater vision, more phenomenal possibilities and an increased desire to change the world, in my special ways. And the more I've become the real me, the less I've needed that motivational 'why' to get me out of bed and into the energy of creation.

Start Where You Are

Wherever you are at right now, please know you can change it, even if right now you feel like an alien with no head. Eight years ago I didn't even want to put my name on the internet. I even started accounts in a pen name so that no-one would be able to find me. (Cute huh?)

And while I was willing to write little things, it took me years to make a video that I was happy to put out publicly and even longer to publish a book. I used to take my friends to networking events because I was too lacking in confidence to go alone. It might be difficult to imagine I was like that if you know me now. 'How can that be?' you might be thinking.

The story is true. I had to start where I could start. So do you. Wherever you are now isn't wrong. It's simply where you are. Every choice you make to take a step forward opens up new possibilities that didn't exist just a moment ago.

You might be thinking that you have to know your purpose, or your 'why' before you can start. Maybe it will take you somewhere. But it's not where you need to start. In the beginning I had a random sense of what I could create in the world, but none of it was really talking to me. If I'd waited to get clear on my 'why' before I started, I'd still be sitting on the starting line, trying to work out what the world is asking of me.

Instead I chose to start creating. I'd had enough of waiting. My mid-life crisis had already had a long, boring and somewhat fruitless 'pre-mid-life-crisis' stage where I'd tried to work out what I'd like to do with the gift of my life. The one thing I knew was that more waiting was a limitation I wasn't willing to settle for!

The only thing that stops us being the brilliance we truly are is the unwillingness to give up the limitations and excuses. If you woke up from the deepest sleep, in a field that stretched forever, not knowing who or where you are, what would you choose? As you wander, absorbing the beauty around you, you discover a blank canvas and the most beautiful paints you've ever seen.

From this moment on, wherever you go, there are hundreds and thousands of these blank canvases, just waiting for you to create. This is the world you live in. There is nothing that is impossible, unless you make it so. You don't have to be part of the inertia epidemic. We'll talk more about your purpose, passion and creating for pleasure in Section 2.

Where Are Your Creative Energies Hiding?

As children we are wonderful creators. We function from inspiration rather than motivation. And at some point most of us stop, often because we buy the idea that we are not creative. We often learn that creativity is about art and craft, not about creating something different! In reality, we're taught that our art and craft should be a certain way to be 'right'. Remember being told 'that's not what a tree looks like!' in art class? In your world, maybe it does! There are over 23,000 varieties of trees in the world... and trillions of possibilities for what you could create. Other people's definitions of creation become the limitations that stop you if you make them real for you.

Have you stopped creating because what you have been creating 'didn't work'? Have you given up trying to work out what will work? Have you wondered what other choices you could make here? All of this is where you give up your creative energies in favour of fitting into the status quo.

What If It's Time To Change The Status Quo?

I know many aware, visionary, creative, inspiring people who are exhausted, disheartened and disillusioned, sometimes taking basic jobs to survive and wondering where it all went 'wrong'. What happened to the promise of 'do what you love and the money will come?' What happened to making choices and creating a life you love?

What happened is the results did not show up fast enough for you, so you decided your ideas didn't work. The moment you go to 'It didn't work', 'I failed', 'This isn't showing up', 'I can't do this', is the moment you stop your requests from coming to life. You begin to hide, or stop

STOP WAITING, START CREATING

yourself, thinking you must be wrong or not capable of creating.

When you stop generating the energy for your ideas and projects by coming to a conclusion about what's not happening, you stop the creative process mid-stream. The Universe hears every point of view you create and it responds according to your choices.

When you stop creating what you desire, the Universe goes 'Oh, you don't want that anymore? Okay, no problem, I'll redirect those resources elsewhere.' And, then the Universe waits to see what else you would like to create. If you keep creating from the idea of 'this isn't working' then that's what you get! Nothing!! If you begin to create something new, the Universe will contribute to that too!

The Universe loves to contribute to what you are creating. Whatever you choose, the big U will support you! Whether it is in your best interests or not! You ask, the Universe delivers (sooner or later!) The only person that can stop the creative process is you! As my friend Dr Dain Heer says "Your point of view creates your reality." And I know you probably don't want to hear that right now. So, before you make yourself wrong for not being able to create what you 'should' be creating, what if you could have gratitude for you, for getting this far? For finding this book. For being willing to explore a different possibility.

What if THIS is the moment that your creative process changes? All it takes is a choice.

The choice… to keep asking for what you would like to have show up, even if nothing looks different on the surface. So many times I've been tempted to give up, and just when I was about to throw everything away, something huge would open up and my ideas would flow into fruition with ease. I wonder how many times you've given up right on the cusp of your success? When it is your time, you'll make the choice to keep going.

The choice... to have no point of view about what shows up. This one is tricky... you've been taught to force your goals into existence by pushing against the flow to make things happen 'your way'. Guess what... force doesn't work! And mostly what you are asking for does show up - just not in the shiny red wrapping and silver ribbon you were expecting. If you reject everything that is not wrapped in the exact packaging you requested, you may be refusing to have something even greater! Often the Universe delivers the underlying energies of your request, rather than the shiny packaging you thought you wanted. Have a look at your life. It will show you exactly what you're asking for. You can change the ask at any time. You can UP the ask at anytime!

The choice... to allow timing to play its role. How many times have you been told 'set a deadline for achieving your goals'? The funny thing is, the Universe doesn't do time. Only people do. Time is an invention. When you try to force timing, it gets ugly. The last time I did this it cost me hundreds of thousands of dollars and two years of my life. At that point I realised it was a good idea to stop forcing my will on the Universe. When other people are involved in what we are asking for, we need to be willing for it to work for everyone's timing, not just ours! (And if you're wondering what to do while you're being infinitely patient, we'll cover that soon.)

The choice... to embrace the good, the bad and the ugly, and to make the most of what is possible with all of it. When we reject everything we haven't judged as good, we reject the

STOP WAITING, START CREATING

hidden possibilities that can come out of our creations not going to plan. In 2014 I planned three trips to Europe. On the first trip so many things changed unexpectedly, that I totally reinvented the business model for Creativity Lab, and totally changed the schedule for the other trips - all within a few days! There were so many gifts in the process, some are still unfolding! If I had been unwilling to be flexible and receive the changes that didn't seem to be so much fun at first, I would never have created something greater.

Creation is 100% about choice. And just in case you are still stopping yourself from creating, we are going to release a few of your (other) favourite excuses for not creating! Please know, you are not alone. I've tried out all of these excuses, and quite a few more, some of them for years on end!

Once I moved beyond my limited self, I began to create greater and greater possibilities for my life and businesses. If a (supposedly) hyper-sensitive, anti-social introvert like me can do it, so can you!! The funny thing is, once I gave up the idea that being sensitive and anti-social was unchangeable, most of my excuses simply disappeared and I began to have a lot more ease with everything. We live in a strange, strange world!

Lisa Murray

'But It's Easy For You...'

There's a myth we need to deal with before we start. I often hear people say to me 'But it's easy for you. You know how to create.' And then they do their best to do it 'my way'. The funny thing is - my way is 'my' way. It probably won't work for you in the way it works for me. Part of this creative adventure you have in Nurturing Ideas Into Life™ is discovering how it is that you create. We truly are all different.

This book offers lots of ideas. You don't have to use them all or even read it in a linear way. Just play with the ones that work for you... or be inspired to create your own. And you'll find that what talks to you one day, won't be so interesting on another day. Every time you read this book you'll see something different! You don't even have to read it chapter by chapter unless you choose to!

Much of my creative process has been discovered as I create. When I'm creating, I sometimes get annoyed... and then I choose to create in a different way, because the old way of creating isn't working for me right now. Creating is an ever-changing process, not a fail-safe recipe that will allow you to be on auto-pilot for the rest of your life.

Creating becomes easier and easier for me and more complicated and more frustrating for most people. Why? Because most people love to make their creations significant. "Look at me. I've created something important!" You may have... and what's next? Are you an Einstein or a Tesla...continuously creating whether the

STOP WAITING, START CREATING

world gives you kudos or not; or are you a one-hit wonder, waiting for the jackpot that never seems to arrive? What's different about my approach to creation and creativity? I create prolifically. Nothing I create is significant - all of it is up for change! And I create for the fun of it, not the outcomes it may (or may not) produce!

For me, creating is like breathing. If I'm not creating I may as well be dead! And if I'm not creating with ease, something needs to change. For most people, creating is something special. Or something you do on a rainy day, when you've run out of options on television or Periscope is having a slow day. Is that true for you? Or do you have a different reality with creating to the average person? Would you like to change or expand the reality you've chosen so far?

One of the most predominant desires on this planet is to retire early so you can do 'nothing'. For many people 'doing nothing' looks a lot like hanging around waiting to die. Is that enough for you? What if your life could be filled with the vibrant energy of continual creation? Did you really come to this beautiful planet to do nothing? Or did you come to explore what else could be possible? To go beyond the boundaries of what has been created before... That is the ease of creation. I make it look easy, because I create non-stop. When you begin to create with awareness of the possibilities that are waiting for you, you'll start making it look easy too!

Lisa Murray

What Is Creation?

Everything!! It's the choices we make and the actions we take that nurture our ideas into reality. It's not just about painting or art. Creation is an energy that runs throughout our life and business in every moment ~ if we will allow it to!

Creation comes in standard flavours, like plain vanilla, or creative flavours... like salted caramel and bacon. Adding creativity to anything you create makes it distinctively yours. It adds your unique view of the world. It brings into existence what has never existed before, in ways that only you can.

Are you creating consciously? Or are you creating from the pretence of non-creation (where you think you aren't creating anything). Take a look at your life. You created it... down to the very last molecule of possibility! If what you have now isn't what you desire, know that it is just the start. What else could you create?

The old movie *It's a Wonderful Life* is a great demonstration of the difference each of us makes far into the future, that we almost never acknowledge. The lead character gets to see what his town would have been like if he hadn't lived there. All of his tiny choices to be different created a huge difference over many years. I wonder if that is true for you too? Even if you have never recognised what it is you create?

When you don't create what you could, the world loses a gift that could contribute to its future. Every

STOP WAITING, START CREATING

moment of your life is a creation... and can be infinitely creative if you will allow it to be! Unless you are trying to fit what you are creating into what already exists in the world. That's the moment you diminish your creative capacities. What could you create that has never existed before?

Creating is the action of bringing your ideas to life. Being creative is bringing your ideas into the world YOUR WAY. It's acknowledging how different you are and allowing your difference to shine through. The world is not asking for another Oprah or Richard Branson. It's asking for YOU!

Creativity isn't about being all arty (although it can be). It's about playing with everything you have and be, and creating something different. It's about making choices to create what does not yet exist. It's about connecting ideas and people in unexpected ways. It's about Nurturing Ideas Into Life™ that have the capacity to change the world.

You have most likely been indoctrinated to believe that change has to be hard. Creation has to be hard... and you definitely can't do it for entertainment and pleasure... or can you?

We think we have to work so hard to get rid of our limitations, and yet, one of the easiest ways to change anything is simply to choose something different! And before you say 'But I can't!' would you be willing to ask if that point of view is true for you?

Was there a time, somewhere in your life, you got so annoyed with the crazy crap you were choosing that you went "Enough! I'm not choosing this anymore!" and that was the end of that limitation? If you've done it once, you can do it again! How much are you asking to change this?

Lisa Murray

A little? A lot? Or totally? When the stakes get high enough, you'll change it - instantly!

STOP WAITING, START CREATING

Not My Circus, Not My Monkeys!

Most of what stops us has nothing to do with us at all. The Polish proverb *'Not My Circus, Not My Monkeys'* offers a super clear hint. Stop listening to the noise of other people's points of view and begin to trust what you know. When you stop buying other people's points of view as real, you begin to create for you!

Would you look at the last few times you agreed with someone else, instead of following what you quietly knew as true in your heart? How did it work out? Is this the moment you can begin to acknowledge that their ideas are no more valuable than yours... and in reality; you know more about your ideas than anyone else?

It is so easy to get trapped in other people's worlds of 'not creating'. How tapped into other people's points of view about creating are you? How many people do you know who are awesome creators? Or are you surrounded by people who are not creating and also do not desire you to create? When you begin creating, it shows other people what's missing in their own life, or it stops them from controlling you with money. For some people, that's an incentive to try putting spokes in your wheel. Are you going to allow that? Or are you ready to choose beyond other people's limitations?

What if you would be willing to create no matter what? 'Get out of my way' is one of my favourite phrases. I rarely say it out loud, but it is inherent in my creative energies! I won't allow anyone or anything to stop me. And often that means saying it to myself!

What do I love about creating? It's an energy that underpins the continual expansion of what is possible with the Universe. It is the platform from which everything we desire can be launched. Without the energy of creation, nothing would exist, not even nature. Have you ever noticed that there have never been two sunrises the same? Our lives could be that creative too if we would be willing to live in a space of constant change and creative possibilities.

To make the world a more wonderful place we have to nurture our ideas. Gently invite them into existence. Without judgement. Without force. Without limiting their brilliance.

If you want to create magic in the world, don't start with why. Start with YOU. It is you that makes the difference. All of your why's are 'strawberries and cream on top' motivation for getting out of bed in the morning. If you have YOU, you'll be more than happy to sprinkle your presence wherever the world needs it. You won't be looking for a reason to get through your struggles. It is likely your struggles will start to disappear!

By the end of this book you will be creating with a lot more ease. Creating from the energies of who you truly be isn't a struggle, it becomes a pleasure, even when nothing is going to plan! What if it is the plan that is incorrect, rather than you being wrong?

WHAT IF... YOU'RE NOT WRONG?

For most of my life I was paralysed by judgement. By whether I was right or wrong. And I was always trying to 'get it right'. If you ever want to wake up and suffer every day, just invoke the power of judgement. Truly, it was a miserable way to live, and it constantly stopped me from creating anything valuable to me or the world.

When you judge something, you limit it to the size of your judgement. It contracts, it becomes smaller and it becomes less than what it can be. How many of your creations have you limited by judging their inadequacies, rather than expanding them by celebrating their possibilities?

As I write this, I'm on a bus between Nottingham and London. In the distance are a church spire and an electricity tower. They are similarly shaped. What makes one beautiful and the other ugly? Nothing except our point of view. Our judgement of what beauty is. Our judgement of what is right and what is wrong.

Imagine finding the true beauty in everything and everyone. Imagine acknowledging the true beauty and brilliance of you. As Gary Douglas, the founder of Access Consciousness® says "What if you are not wrong... what if you are just different?" That was my mantra for a long time, especially when people close to me were judging me non-stop!

If you would be the difference you are, instead of making it wrong, because you can't see anyone else being that different, would your capacity for creating expand further than you have imagined possible?

In the increasingly rare moments when my creative energies are being gobbled up by the judgement monster, I've discovered that taking my creations into nature is a wonderful antidote. Nature doesn't judge. It just is. When you are out in nature by yourself, you are present with the energy of non-judgement. In nature you begin to know what your points of view are about your creations, and what the perspectives are that other people live and judge by. The perspectives that other people have will be less present in the space that nature offers. What if you would stop judging your creations? What would be different?

Without judgement, our creations can be received by far more people. Think of it this way.... When someone is desperate, there is an energy that you don't want to be near. It's more than a little repulsive! When someone is judging you, it's the same. You'd rather keep your distance! When you judge your creations, can they contribute to you? Or do people tend to stay away from what you are creating too?

STOP WAITING, START CREATING

If you wake up and everything you created yesterday (and the day before... and the day before... and...) is 'WRONG'... you've just uncreated everything you had begun to create. Is this what keeps you going around in circles, never quite finishing anything? Can you see where 'stuck' could be coming from?

You are aware of what other people think. Mostly you are allowing yourself to be stopped by other people's judgements and criticisms. At an Access Consciousness® conference I discovered that people only judge you for what they have been or done themselves. This changed my life beyond measure - I realised I was making other people's points of view significant - and they were actually nothing to do with me! So for every judgement you are aware of, everywhere you have been there, done that, or judged that or been judged for it, would you uncreate and destroy it all now? These are old patterns that aren't worth perpetuating into your future!

What if you could be grateful for the information people give you about themselves when they judge you? One of my co-creators accidentally copied me in on an email to a class participant. She criticised my co-ordinator and I in some detail, and then proceeded to announce how she would just create something similar to what I was doing, for 'her people'.

I replied to the email in a very polite and detached way, with some additional clarity on the situation. If someone is so devoid of ideas that they need to copy mine, good luck with that! What was interesting was I'd been asking some questions about what went on with the classes she had been creating, as there was clearly something that wasn't working. I got exactly the

43

information I was asking for. The Universe is truly amazing like that!

What was the gift in this judgement? I didn't buy it as true or real... I just went "Thank you for the information! How does it get better than this?" The fastest way to remove the impact of judgement on you and your life, is to have gratitude instead. If you were grateful for every judgement that came your way, your capacity to receive everything (including money) would be exponentialised beyond your wildest dreams!

On my naughty days I say to people: "Oh wow, you're being judgemental again. I hope it's making you happy! Have a nice day!" with a huge grin on my face. And then I go out and have a good time somewhere else. I used to take judgement so personally - and then I got to see that it's not true and it's not real. It's just their point of view. And when you find their judgement amusing rather than upsetting, it messes with their reality in so many ways! Imagine what you could create if judgement never had the power to stop you ever again?

People will judge you as a way of trying to keep you small. They don't want you to leave their nice cosy tiny world. You have to be willing to choose what will work for you. Are you asking for people who will contribute to you being more? Or people who like to keep you exactly as you are? If ever anyone says 'don't change' to you, you know what's going on!! It's not a compliment! You don't need to be perfect for anyone else. Being infinitely creative is way more fun!

Allowing yourself the space of no judgement is a muscle you build. It's an energy you be in each moment that becomes an invitation for people to connect with you. What energy can you BE with people to be the catalyst for change that you and your ideas have the capacity for? Have you ever watched Russell Brand being interviewed? He's a great example of someone who never buys judgement about himself. He invites people to question what they think they know. I wonder if expressing your ideas in the world could create that possibility too?

Positive Judgment Is Still Judgement

In the movie 'Divergent' people have to choose one faction and limit themselves to a specific set of skills and capacities for the rest of their life. It's positive judgement at its worst. 'Show me your best limited self and you can be included' was the message. If they don't choose because they would like to be everything they truly are, they become outcasts and they are sent to live on the edges of a world that controls everything through limitation.

How often is this replicated in our society? To me, there's a different kind of FIFO operating… it's not "Fly In, Fly Out" (for the Aussies) or "First In, First Out" (for the rest of the world) - it's "Fit In or Fuck Off", and it's not a contribution to being the creators of magnitude we truly are. What could be different in the world if we would start to include people for their brilliance, rather than excluding them for their unwillingness to fit in to the limitations most people live by?

When I first went to school I was very confused. The teacher would show us how to do something and I would

Lisa Murray

always be able to see another possibility, which was usually faster and easier. And rather than be acknowledged for my creativity and awareness, I was made wrong for not following the instructions. It took me a long time to acknowledge that I probably knew more than the teacher. This is how we learn to limit our creative capacities.

Did you learn to make your creations into 'nothing'? Did you get in trouble for being too excited about what you were creating? Did you learn that nothing you create has value? Or did you learn that creating is fun, joyful and a contribution to everyone around you? Whatever you learned, it's just a judgement. If you had no point of view, you would have the continual energy of unlimited creation.

Buying the positive judgements as real can work you over even more than believing a negative judgement. Have you noticed that when you are told you are great at something, you often go into resistance? 'Who me? That can't be right. I'm no good at anything...' and then we dismiss the very capacities we could be using to create. How many times has someone acknowledged you or your talent, and you've immediately stopped creating? Crazy huh? Are you willing to stop stopping you now?

I remember the comment "Lisa has lots of potential but she doesn't apply herself" on almost every report card I ever received at school. Yes, I found school more than a little boring. Even then I was an awesome multi-tasker, always having a book hidden nearby so I could read if what the teacher was talking about wasn't interesting to me. People project our 'potential' at us, while judging us for fulfilling it - all at the same time. It's no wonder we get confused and begin to hide our capacities to create!

STOP WAITING, START CREATING

"If you are irritated by every rub, how will you be polished?" ~ **Rumi**

What are you unwilling to receive about your talents, capacities and abilities? Are you willing to know how amazing you are?

Potential is seen as something wonderful, and actually it is something that never shows up. Potential is all about judging what is possible in the future. Deciding in advance if you can... or if you can't!. How do you know until you start? What if you would keep asking for possibilities to show up instead of making decisions that you have to stick to?

What is it you are not willing to receive about the brilliance of you; that if you would receive it, would change everything? What if you are way more amazing than you've ever allowed yourself to know? We tend to compare our brilliance to the most amazing people we know and then always find ourselves lacking. It's that insane thing of comparing someone else's public image to our private life and always coming up as 'less than'. Is that a way to create more or is it a limited choice that keeps us creating nothing?

There's one more thing we need to talk about here. Remember the idea that you only judge someone else for something if you have already been it or done it, in this or some other lifetime? So if you are judging your kids or your partner or your friend for not living up to their potential... I wonder what else is possible for you right now? How much unused potency and potential are you hiding away?

One of the biggest things for me has been to get to a space where I'm willing to receive judgement. I spent so much time and energy avoiding judgement, and then I realised this. If no-one is judging you or if nothing you say is at all controversial, then you are impacting no-one and you are not making a difference.

If no-one is even noticing what you are creating… you are not even a blip on the radar of the world. Oops! Imagine the impact you could make in the world if you would create something that would black out their radar instead?

Would that be more fun for you than exhausting yourself by constantly hiding your brilliance? Are you a swan trying to pretend you are an ugly duckling? Are you hiding from the foxes and hawks instead of unfurling your wings and showing the world your beauty? This is not the time to hide your brilliance. Those times are gone. The world is asking for you NOW!

If you are not sure if this is you… do you wear clothes to fit in rather than stand out? Do you keep quiet when you are aware of exactly what is required? Do you undercharge people because (you think) they can't afford it? Do you hangout backstage in support roles rather than being the leader you truly are? What would you have to be or do different to black out the judgement radar and take over the world?

****** EXPLORATION ******

If you would like to stop being at the effect of other people's judgements, the fastest way is to be grateful for

STOP WAITING, START CREATING

every single crazy point of view... and to start to find them funny. If you're not quite there yet, you may like to unravel some of the judgements that are stopping you.

What one judgement stops you every single time? Look at the energy of your life with that judgement and then look at it without that judgement. Can you (and will you) create something greater if you stop buying the lies that that particular judgement is creating?

The funny thing is, there really isn't a 'how'. It's just a choice, a demand you make of you. "Whenever people judge me for _____ I will not buy it as true or real ever again." That's how simple it is to change this!

You know YOU better than anyone. Take the last ten judgements you have received and ask "Is this true for me?" If not, would you let it all go without another thought? Hint: if you have some doubt, it is probably not true for you; it is the lingering wafts of other people's projections of what or who you are. Isn't it so cool that they care so much!!?

Or would it be even cooler if you cared for you so much that no-one else's point of view would matter more than your own? And please be clear, I'm not suggesting you become a Nancy-Know-It-All, I'm suggesting you value what you know about you and your ideas!

Now... what are you grateful to YOU for? Are you grateful for everything you have chosen? Are you grateful for your beauty, your creativity, your capacity for change? Write down at least 100 things you are grateful to you for! Are you way more phenomenal than you've ever allowed yourself to imagine?

If you'd like to have a No Judgement Day, start by being grateful for everything you are, everything you are aware of, everything you have created and everything that is yet to be created. And watch your creative energies expand!

On an adventure in South Africa, I booked some accommodation on a nature reserve where the zebras, giraffes and wildebeest roam freely between the huts. When I arrived the resort was somewhat more run-down than the pictures showed. The room was smelly, the shower didn't work and the restaurant was filthy. My first response was to make myself wrong for the questions I had not asked. It is crystal clear that I don't like to slum it!!

After an hour of misery I stopped. I asked for a new room (which was so much better than the first one) and then I got some wine and relaxed with an energetically created meditation designed to change your reality, which I played all night. I was in the question about whether I would go somewhere else the next day. When I woke to birdsong, impala and kittens outside my door, a stunning view of the lake through the trees and a deep sense of peace, I chose to stay for the second night. I spontaneously set up work-camp with a mattress on the patio and had a delightful day editing this book! And I was grateful for the choice to be continually in the question of what would actually work for me, with no right or wrong involved.

If you had total gratitude for yourself, what could you allow you to be or do different today? Would you be exuberant? Would you be playful? Would you be kind? Would you be creative? Would you be wealthy? Would you be spontaneous? Would you be curious? Who would you be? Being more 'you' is the foundation for creating more.

WHAT'S STOPPING YOU?

Most people think that if they define a problem, they have to solve it before they can move forward. We've been taught that identifying and solving problems is valuable and most of us are so very brilliant at it that we often create another problem once we solve the first one. It's a very creative approach to stopping yourself from ever getting anywhere! Ever noticed? Let's solve a few of the most common 'problems' first. At the very least it will give you a clearer space to create from!

When I had jobs, I was stupid enough to write 'problem-solver' on my resume. Guess what kind of jobs I always got? Yes… ones with huge problems that no-one else wanted to tackle. The funny thing is, it was easy for me to solve problems, it just wasn't that much fun. We're taught that our value is in solving problems. But is it? What if our value could be in creating with elegance and ease?

Imagine a world where job advertisements ask for applicants who love to make things happen with ease!

Wouldn't that be bliss? There's one way to create that world. Start choosing that in your life and your work today. We could start a movement. 'Give up your trauma and drama, and create with ease.' Wanna play?

Another choice is to see nothing as a problem. To look at so-called obstacles and go 'well that's interesting!' and throw the obstacles away. You could also stop creating the challenges that prove how brilliant you are when you solve them... but that would be way too easy. You would have too much fun creating with ease.

Because you're reading this book, I'm guessing you could have this weird idea that you need to do it the hard way! Is that true? Or is it your time to stop wading through shit? Or maybe you'd love to keep your trauma and drama... in which case, please stop reading now and give this book to someone who would love to create for the fun of it!

So what is stopping you? Are you ready for a different choice now? I hope so, because we're going to dive right into all of the excuses you use to stop you. And we're going to let them go. One by one... Gently release them so that you can create with ease.

Creating is a choice. It sometimes takes courage. Mostly it takes a willingness to be who we truly are. Not who other people have told us we are. (Ever noticed there is a really huge gap between these two things?)

It takes a choice to stop being limited and start being limitless. That is the only real difference between me and the limitations I used to think were me. So... let's play!

"But I'm Not Creative"

I started my first business at eight. When I was fourteen I knew I would have my own businesses "one day". At 39 (and after three rounds of burnout) I was still working for other people, the lure of a regular pay check keeping my true desires unmet.

What was stopping me? I couldn't come up with a business idea that I loved. Yes, truly... it happens to even the most creative of us! At 40 the burnout was so intense my body kicked me out of my job. Not being able to sit up for more than three hours at a time has its limitations. And so I embarked on an entrepreneurial adventure - one without plans! I'm still not sure if that was brave or just plain crazy!

What I discovered was that most of my creative energy was being used up on other people's projects (i.e. my employers). I had heaps of creative ideas and inspiration at work. And once I unwound myself from the demands of having a job I created enough space for those energies to show up for me and my projects. And that's not to say you have to quit your job to create. You don't. You just have to create the space for creating.

The first thirty business ideas I had were terrible. The next thirty were slightly better. And after about 300 ideas I started a business that I closed a month later because I very quickly realised it couldn't take me where I knew I could go.

Lisa Murray

The next adventure I chose was business coaching - and I'm still running that business seven years later, although by the time you read this, I will have merged it with Creativity Lab. What started as BlissTribe also became Creativity Lab, four years after I was aware of the energy of the business and what it could create in the world. Now I have one business and over thirty creation projects, as well as more books in the pipeline. Creating never shows up how we think it will.

For each of these businesses, there was no clear path for creating. I discovered that each choice I made would lead me somewhere else. Each choice I made showed me a heap of other possibilities I could choose from. If you are waiting for a gorgeous gold-paved path to success, to miraculously open up before you, please know there isn't one, unless you create it with your choices! To expand your creative capacities, you have to be willing to take the thousand tiny steps into the unknown. You have to be willing to be different.

Are you aware that you see the world in unusual ways? Do you know you are different? Or is your difference so normal to you that you think everyone is just like you? I often talk about ideas that are so normal to me it's like breathing. And people look at me like I have two heads - eventually someone explains they never saw it that way before! What is normal to you is not normal to other people.

The good news is - you are different! You have just spent most of your life trying to fit in. When you stop fitting in, you start to become aware of how different you are. Once you start to acknowledge your difference, you'll never lack ideas again. What do you know, that no-one else is sensing yet? Have you ever had an idea that you did nothing about... and then you got really annoyed because someone else put the idea into the world? If that's you, you don't have a lack of creative ideas, you have a lack of timing and action.

Are you making yourself wrong for what you are aware of? Imagine if you stopped doing that. Stopped second-guessing yourself. Stopped doubting your ideas. Nothing changes if you don't start to create what you know is possible. You always know! More on this in Section Two - What Are You Creating?

"I Haven't Got Time"

Using time as an excuse is not your best creation. Whether it's your kids, your partner, your three other jobs or your manic capacity for discovering new ideas, it's easy to blame 'no time' for what you aren't creating. I was really great at making time my enemy, until I heard Nobel Prize winning American novelist, professor and single mother Toni Morrison talk about writing at the edges of her day.

She meant take whatever time you have, even if it is only ten minutes, and create! Ellsworth Kelly sketched on a bus every day. I sometimes make sweet little watercolour sketches at my desk while I'm on the phone with people. It gives my hands something to do! You don't need three hours to prepare and another three hours to actually create. It is our ideas about what creating 'should' be, that stop us from creating in every spare two minutes we have. Who says you can't come up with ideas while in a queue

Lisa Murray

at the bank? Who says you can't speed write while your enjoyable other is in the shower?

You can be creative in just a few minutes. And if you commit to your creative process, even if it is ten minutes when you wake up and ten minutes just before you sleep, you will create!

This simple idea revolutionised my creative output. It made me infinitely more productive. Not because I suddenly found more time, but because I saw how fruitless it was to use time as an excuse for not creating. If you have the desire to create, you just need to start, even if it is in the three minutes while you are waiting to collect the kids from school. Creating can happen anywhere.

It is actually not time we need for creating, but space. Many famous artists, musicians and writers were brilliant because they found the space to create (sometimes through alcohol or drugs… naturally there are other choices!) They arranged their lives in ways that allowed for space. What can you change that would give you more space for creating?

Space is where you expand your energy rather than focus it. Where you allow your creative capacities to show up however they can, rather than demanding they fit to time-lines. If the only clear space you can find is at 2am, you'll choose it if you truly desire to create. I love creating when everyone else is asleep or when I'm way out in the wilds of nature. I create way faster! Space is where you create the environment for creating that works for you. No matter what! You don't allow the world to impinge on your space. With space, we create with a lot more ease.

Space can be created in many different ways. What are the activities you are slow at, that if you delegated or outsourced them to someone else, would turn your life into a flowing stream of creative bliss? For everything you detest doing, there is someone else who loves it and is way better at it than you! Isn't it so cool how the Universe creates so much variety so that every single one of us can enjoy life?

Whether you are a small business owner, a senior executive or a parent, there often isn't enough space to eat lunch, let alone create the luxury of space to ponder new possibilities - or is there? What you create is a choice. If the first thing you create is space for creating and creativity, you are honouring you by allowing your life to unfold as it can. There is **research**[1] showing that a two hour lunch break will make you more productive than working non-stop. (See? I knew exactly what I was doing when I went on those boozy corporate lunches ;))

What would be different in your life if you put you and your ideas first?

Spontaneous creation is a great space to begin creating because you don't have time to put all your excuses and resistances in place. It's being present in the moment: 'Here's a space for creation, let's play!' Instead of planning it out, and then going into the all too seductive but, infinitely unproductive energy of 'I have to… but I don't feel like it right now.'

So, right now, put down this book and go create something spontaneously, just for the fun of it, because you can, with no particular outcome required. How different would your life be if you bounced from creation to creation spontaneously? Could the energy of creation begin to flow throughout every choice you make?

Lisa Murray

And if your mind is drawing a blank about what you could create spontaneously, start an ideas list and for each project, write down at least three 'first steps' you could take. When you desire a spontaneous creation break, play with whatever feels the most fun from this list. It's a 'to-create' list, not a to-do list. They are worlds apart in the invitation they are to your creative energies!

"I've Lost My Creative Edge"

Did you used to be creative? Wondering where all that inspiration went? What if how you used to create was great for that time and space, and now there is a new way for you to be creative in the world?

I love change. I embrace it. I seek it. And every few months, my entire process for creating undergoes a huge metamorphosis. Yes. Every. Few. Months. ...Sometimes. Even. Faster! It's exhilarating if you are willing to let go of the terror of "oh wow... I don't know how to write like I did yesterday."

When I wake up and my Universe has changed dynamically I ask questions. What worked last week doesn't do it for me anymore. The first time it happened I was a bit surprised. And I adapted quite quickly. Since then, it's been an adventure, if not always a comfortable one! I'm curious about how many different ways there are to create and be creative. So I never perceive it as a loss. It's always a gift. Other people might call this having a creative block. I call it an adventure. And so it never becomes a block in my world.

What it shows me is, how much my possibilities are shifting and changing. How much I'm willing to be out-of-control. How much I'm willing to lose sight of the edges of reality, so that I can discover something beyond what has existed before. How much my abilities and talents and capacities for creation are expanding in every moment.

So if you are wailing about your creative muse going missing, maybe there's greater inspiration just waiting for you to open your senses! What if things like 'writers block' don't truly exist? What if they are an invention... a very limited way of describing what happens when our creative process continually changes?

How do you discover what's possible? You play with your creative process! Every day. And you allow it to evolve. You are not the same person you were yesterday. Is it going to create a different future if you try to create from the same space? Or could you create something much more amazing if you create from the energy of who you are right now? More on that in Section Three - Exploring Your Creative Process!

"I'm Waiting..."

This is the excuse that most of us love most. It's the part of the book you are most likely to get uncomfortable with. It can be momentarily confronting when someone names our favourite excuse and then takes it away. Please read this and relax. You aren't wrong. This entire book is designed to nurture you through the discomfort of waiting. Don't stop reading right when the change you are asking for is going to become possible! What is on the other side is worth a little temporary discomfort. Are you ready? It's time to be brave!

Have you ever caught yourself saying "I'll create that when…"? It's a form of waiting, of procrastination, of stopping you from being you! Where is it you are waiting, before you will start your idea or project?

◆ *For the right person (or people) to show up?*

◆ *For the right moment to quit your job?*

◆ *For the right set of circumstances to be in place?*

◆ *For enough money to be available for your dreams?*

◆ *For people to catch up with you? (They may never choose that!)*

◆ *For people to hear you or your message?*

◆ *For the stars and the planets to line up?*

◆ *For someone's approval?*

◆ *For the one magic 'thing' that will fix everything? (Lotto anyone?)*

◆ *For everything to be fixed first?*

◆ *To feel inspired (where is that creative muse hiding? Hint… YOU are your muse!)*

STOP WAITING, START CREATING

◆ *To have an idea worth putting energy into?*

◆ *To find the time to create?*

◆ *To be the person you need to be before you start?*

◆ *To get over your fears?*

◆ *To be chosen?*

◆ *For a sign? (Or for a set of three signs, because then it MUST be right!)... What if you truly do KNOW what you know? What if waiting for three signs is a way of slowing yourself down?*

What is it YOU are waiting for... or waiting to be? Make a list right now... and then ask yourself "Is this real? Or is it an excuse I'm using to stop myself? If all of this showed up in the next ten minutes, what would actually change? Or would I find another list of things to wait for?"

Mostly these are just the stories and lies we tell ourselves. I used to be so angry at the world that I couldn't create, that my creations weren't working... And now I know the anger was just awareness of the lies I was telling myself. None of it was true. When I made the demand of myself to start creating consistently, everything changed. When you get honest with yourself, everything shows up differently! Stick with me here, by the end of this book, your situation will be changing with ease. Truth, can any of these things on your list stop you? Or is it you stopping you?

Lisa Murray

I've discovered that if I make the demand of myself to constantly be moving forward, it has the effect of parting the Red Sea. Nothing and no-one can get in my way. Possibilities show up where there weren't any! Ideas flow faster than I can capture them. I become immersed in choices, rather than waiting! Is it comfortable? Not always. But it sure beats waiting!

Much of the great, amazing stuff in the world is created from a space of being uncomfortable. Just because change isn't comfortable doesn't mean we shouldn't demand it of ourselves.

What are you putting BEFORE your creations? "I will but... I will when... I will after...". If I waited until I had the money to take Creativity Lab overseas, I'd still be sitting in Australia, wondering how to get it happening. The first time I took Creativity Lab overseas it was to Sweden. I left on a week's notice, knowing that Paypal had frozen my account and all the class payments were in that account. You could call it a cash-flow crisis.

I went anyway. I knew that somehow it would work. It took a bit of courage to get on the plane not knowing how I would pay for everything - fortunately people continued to book and we asked them to pay in cash. And I did some private coaching sessions too. So it all worked out perfectly in the end. When you are choosing to do something, know there is ALWAYS a way!!! You just need to be creative enough to find it.

There is not just 'one thing' that, if it changes, will allow you to be creative. There are a thousand small things you can change that will allow you to begin creating right now. Any one of them can be a starting point. You just have to start. A simple way to begin is to do something different. If you normally ask people what they think, make a choice by yourself and see where it leads. If you normally lead, sit back and observe what others offer. If you normally follow, speak up. If you normally wait for your ideas to be chosen, choose what you desire instead. These tiny choices become the big choices that allow us to move beyond waiting.

Waiting does not create comfort! We think it does...... and yet mostly it is waiting that makes us increasingly uncomfortable. Because somewhere deep inside, we know we're not on a path that will take us where we'd like to go. The paradox is, whatever we choose, it takes us somewhere.

There are some moments where there is a stillness with your projects, rather than a resistance. This is the time to allow yourself some space to chill-out, before the next flurry of activity. That kind of 'waiting' is different. It's not waiting. It's allowing the Universe to co-create with you. It's allowing timing to do its glorious thing. You'll know the difference, you just have to ask!

"No-one Is Interested In What I Have To Offer"

It's so easy to let doubt get in the way of being a contribution to the world. If you've ever found yourself thinking: "Who am I to be a voice? What have I got to offer? Who would want to listen to me? Maybe I'm a fraud" then you know exactly what I'm talking about! Doubt is a trigger that we use to distract ourselves from creating. When we stop giving doubt value, our capacity to create changes dynamically.

When I first quit my job I had no idea that anyone would value what I knew. Because I have always created from a very different space, I was used to being judged for how I created. I thought my creative process was wrong. And so I didn't see any value in talking about it.

Gary Douglas, from Access Consciousness® asks "What if your wrongness is your strongness?" When I first heard this I had no idea what it meant. How could being wrong be a strength? As people started asking me about how I create, I realised that the very thing I made myself so wrong for, is actually the thing people are looking for! Yes, we live on a strange and funny planet. Nothing is as we believe it to be.

The mantra of "I'm not wrong, I'm just different" stops me from always seeing my way as wrong. And it started a process of acknowledging how many people could have the change they are asking for, if I would talk about how I'm different. I'm sure this is only true for me... it could never apply to you! Or could it?

You have to move past the conundrum of 'If no-one is talking about this I must be wrong. And if everyone is talking about this, there is nothing else I can say.' Neither of these statements are true. If you have a sense of what you would like to say, and you say it in a way that is unique to you, there will be people who need to hear that message in that way. You have to trust your knowing!

What is it that is so easy for you that you find it ridiculous that other people can't do it? That beautiful thing is a great place to start your creative adventures. When other people find something difficult, that to you is simple, you have something to teach, something to invite

STOP WAITING, START CREATING

others to. Even if you think you don't know how to teach it.

Writing is like that for me. It's so natural for me to write to the energy of what is going on that I would just do it, without even knowing what I was doing. When people started persistently asking me to teach them to write, I was confused. Spelling and grammar is not really my thing. Once I realised they desired to write to the energy, I was even more confused. How do you teach something when your 'how' is so intangible?

One simple way forward is that you invite people to ask you questions about your process - and you record the insights you offer them. Once you've done that for a while, your process will start to become tangible to you and valuable to others. Yes... creating can be that easy!

How do you get rid of the doubt? There are lots of ways. One of my favourites is to ask the Universe to show you what you contribute, beyond doubt.

I once had a boyfriend who was constantly judging me for not being a contribution to him or the relationship. It was exhausting for me. So I left him for a week and I took all of my energy out of his Universe. After two days he called me up crying. "I miss you and I'd like you to come back... blah blah blah." But apparently I was no contribution to him! Much!!!!! You can't believe what people say. You have to trust you and trust what you know. And yes, in case you are wondering, that was the beginning of the end. It's no fun being with someone who judges you non-stop.

{Side-note: For YOU... creative, brilliant being that you are... the person who judges you non-stop may be you... have you ever considered being kinder to yourself?

Lisa Murray

It's a lot easier than always trying to be someone you are not!!}

Whatever you create touches others far beyond what you have ever acknowledged. My friend Dr Dain Heer gave me this great question. Ask the Universe to show you everywhere you are the ripple effect, everywhere you have made a difference...

> *"Universe, would you show me where I'm a contribution please?"*

The first time I asked this, I had people 'randomly' calling me and writing to me about conversations we had enjoyed years previously. Telling me about what I'd said to them and how it had made a difference or changed their life dynamically. I was so surprised! I did not even really remember what we had talked about, and I had no idea they had taken anything useful from the conversation. So please, never underestimate your contributions.

Now I have a greater sense of the possibilities of contribution… and I ask for the fun of it. To get a sense of what I've been creating that I am not yet aware of. It's a cool game to play with the Universe!! And it's a fast way to get over doubt.

When you truly begin to receive the contribution you are (as opposed to the contribution you have judged yourself for not being) you'll wake up inspired to create. You won't be looking for external validation or acknowledgement of what you offer the world as your motivation for creating.

Being a contribution doesn't make you special. It just allows you to show up as you in the world. Most of us

STOP WAITING, START CREATING

avoid being special or standing out from the crowd as we know it comes with lots of judgement. What if you would be willing to receive the judgement? If you'd like to make a lot more money, you have to be willing to have people judge you.

In Australia we stop ourselves from being all we can be due to the Tall Poppy Syndrome - where conspicuous success is envied, criticised and judged so that people are 'cut down to size'. There is a similar point of view in Canada, but not America. In the Scandinavian countries there is a similar construct - it's called the Law of Jante - or Janteloven in Danish or Norwegian and Jantelagen in Swedish.

The Law of Jante[2] was discussed in the fiction book *A Fugitive Crosses His Tracks* by Axsel Sandemose. It is a great description of how most people currently live. It goes like this:

1. *You're not to think you are anything special.*

2. *You're not to think you are as good as we are.*

3. *You're not to think you are smarter than we are.*

4. *You're not to convince yourself that you are better than we are.*

5. *You're not to think you know more than we do.*

6. *You're not to think you are more important than we are.*

7. *You're not to think you are good at anything.*

8. *You're not to laugh at us.*

Lisa Murray

9. You're not to think anyone cares about you.

10. You're not to think you can teach us anything.

Great list huh? Never allow an individual to be the greatness they are! No wonder we try not to stand out from the crowd!

Jantelagen shows up when people judge you for being an individual, for being different, for being an achiever or successful. Like those things are wrong? How can 'being you' be wrong? It can't unless you allow it! Are you ready to stop fitting into the collective limitations that everyone else buys as true and real? Is it time for ALL of your creative brilliance to shine?

When you allow other people's points of view to limit what you are willing to create, you stop the world from changing, from being greater. Just because they are not willing to see beyond their limited points of view. Contribution is contribution - whether it is for individual or collaborative success - there is nothing that makes one wrong and the other right, except for the point of view we choose to hold onto. Are you willing to change everything that is creating those points of view now?

Are you still doubting the value of what you know? Start some conversations with people. Open up some discussions where you get to see what people know about your topic. Do you have something different to offer? Are people curious about your ideas? Are they asking you questions? If so, this is the start of knowing who your 'most fun people' are. If not, spread your wings further… ask the Universe to show you where 'your people' are hanging out. And have those conversations again. Your doubts will diminish as you find the people who are seeking you. It doesn't mean you own them, it means you get to play with the people who desire what you are offering.

One more thing... the greatest antidote to doubt is an innate knowing that you are brilliant at your thing. You have gifts. Use them! Don't pretend or try to be something you're not. Have you noticed how not fun that is?

"I Don't Know Enough to Start - I'm a Fraud!"

A lot of people come to me for coaching with this idea they have to get an education before they begin their business. They assume the certificates on the wall will create their business. It's almost never true. But those certificates are a wonderful way of proving that you have learned what you already knew!

I did an MBA because my job required it. I can think of a lot of ways I could have put that time and money to better use from a business perspective; and I'm really grateful for the amazing friends I made! If you are using education as a crutch, rather than a contribution to what you are creating, there are other, faster ways to get where you are going! And this is not a rant against education - I spend thousands every year on increasing my awareness, and that has a big payoff in my business and life.

Choosing education that will add to your capabilities is different to choosing education that will add to your office decor.

A certificate does not stop you from feeling like a fraud. Being amazing at what you do and acknowledging it does. You have to ask the question: "If I choose this, what will it create?" rather than go to the conclusion that going to yet another training will be the panacea to end all doubt!

The fastest way to learn what you need to know is to dive-in. To start working with clients. To start writing. To start coding. To start creating. To take just the first step. As you create, you'll discover where your knowledge gaps are. That's the time to choose to learn more. Not when you are trying to prop yourself up to get started! (Of course, this does not apply to every profession - if you are a doctor or a lawyer, for example, you need to meet the appropriate regulations.)

If you are resisting the start, be willing to fail. Be willing for it all to go pear-shaped. Be willing for it to be an adventure, rather than an exercise in perfection. I learn something new every time I facilitate a class or a person. I learn more every time I launch a new program or write another book. I never have the point of view I have to get it right. I just need to show up and do the best I can. And what I've discovered is that 99% of the time, that is far more than enough!

The really cool thing is, whatever you know, you only need to be a few steps ahead of the people you are working with. You don't need to know everything before you start! And you don't need to fake it until you make it. Show up, contribute what you can, and charge a fair price for what you're offering. The only times people will get pissed with you is if you overcharge them or give them more than they are willing to receive. Deliver great value and you'll be on your way! The only times you'll get

STOP WAITING, START CREATING

pissed off or resentful is when you aren't charging what you are worth or working with the people that you can contribute the most to.

Are you willing to receive a true sense of what you DO know? I went through a phase where my answer to most questions about what I was creating was 'I don't know'. One day, a mentor said to me: 'Those three words are exactly what is stopping you from creating and having everything you desire.' I was confused, how could that be? If I knew, I wouldn't be asking!! The funny thing is, that's not how it works.

I realised the fastest way to find out would be to stop saying 'I don't know'. That was a lot harder than I expected. I was saying it a lot!!! Within a few weeks I had trained myself to ask a question instead. "Good question, what do I know here?' became my new 'fallback' answer. And with that question, has come so much information. If I'd instituted an 'I don't know' swear jar, I'd have become richer than Richard Branson, probably within hours. My mentor was spot on in more ways than the obvious. A couple of years down the track I'm acknowledging just how much I am aware of the future. Telling myself 'I don't know' was cutting all of that information and awareness off.

You know way more than you imagine. You just have to be willing to acknowledge what you know. Every time someone compliments you, or you are aware of how something is going to turn out, or you have a brilliant idea, you need to acknowledge your awareness. Not only will you expand what you know, but the 'I don't know (enough)' trap cannot contain you any longer! We'll explore this more in Section 2 - in the Creating Isn't Logical chapter!

Lisa Murray

"I'm Scared of Being Visible"

Around eight years ago, I went to a friend's meditation night and she took us on a wild and trippy journey into the future. There were no drugs, just huge amounts of awareness!

Trippy? When you see yourself talking to an audience of thousands and you are an introvert with burnout, that's enough to send you seeking a different planet! I was petrified! And I'm so grateful for the information, as it sent me seeking a different future, changing my life beyond recognition, in ways I never imagined possible!

At that time, I had quite a terror of being seen. I would do anything to avoid public speaking, even though my MBA colleagues would always nominate me to speak because I was 'good at it'. (I definitely did not believe them - I figured they didn't want to do it any more than I did and were manipulating me into it!).

I was also entertaining myself coming up with pen names so I'd never have to use my real name on the internet. I did not have a single photograph of myself that I was happy to put out publicly (and I was so anxious about having my photo taken that I did not see a possibility for getting new photos anytime soon!).

Yes... I was a basket-case of invisibility, hiding in any dark corner I could find, which is funny in hindsight, as I had often chosen jobs that were about leading people and projects.

STOP WAITING, START CREATING

If "my dream is too big and if it comes true, I'll have to put myself out in the world" is the single thing stopping you from creating, please know that anything can change if you will allow it to! I am living proof! For me, changing it took quite a few advanced Access Consciousness® classes - there were a lot of unconscious decisions to change! And there are some shortcuts I can share with you now, using the amazing tools I learned.

Firstly, are you scared, anxious, terrified and petrified... or are you wildly excited? Physiologically these energies are the same. I realised I was excited, not petrified! That one awareness changed my life dynamically! How much fun can you have with this? Right now, take anything you've been saying 'I'm scared about ....and replace it with 'I'm excited about...' - Which one feels lighter and more expansive (or makes you giggle!)? That's the one that's true for you!

Secondly, have you asked the question 'Who does this belong to?' What if you are way more psychic than you acknowledge? What if you're aware of other people's realities - their thoughts, feelings and emotions? If you've ever been described as over-sensitive, consider that you may be far more aware than the average bear! With this awareness, you pick up on other people's points of view and you think they are yours... after all, they are in your head right?

The simple solution to this, is to ask: "Is this mine?" for all thoughts, feelings and emotions. 99.99999% of the mush in your head is not yours. How do I know this? I have busy-brain; over-thinking is way too natural for me. I once went way out in the country for the weekend, with no other people around, the entire rabble in my head just stopped. It was quiet in there! And then, as we drove back into the city, I could hear all the noise getting louder and louder. What the…???

It was magic to me. I realised most of the craziness in my head was nothing to do with me. Not the doubt, the fear, the shame, the guilt, the low self-esteem or even the tiredness… none of it! So now I am constantly in the question, asking: "Is this mine?" If it lightens up and there is more space showing up then say, "Return to sender with consciousness attached" and you won't have to keep buying any of those ideas as real anymore! My brain is so much more peaceful now - I can even walk through a city and have just my awareness, not a trillion ADHD thoughts about everything. That's what I call bliss!

The third tool that allowed me to move into being more visible with ease was a question Access Consciousness® co-creator Dr Dain Heer asked me: "What if being famous could be totally different than what you already know about it?" That idea opened up a lot of space for me. I realised I could create being visible my way - and that it didn't mean having to become an overnight extrovert driving the fame train! How many points of view do you have about what being visible means? If none of those ideas are true, what would you like to choose?

The fourth tool is about being able to receive other people's judgement without having a point of view. As I've already mentioned, judgement can be positive or negative. I've seen people get stuck when they've been acknowledged for their success, just as much as getting stuck for being judged for not succeeding. When you allow all judgements to be an interesting point of view, you don't buy any of them as real. That's another version of bliss!

Oh yeah... and what if failure is not real either? What if it is just another invention that keeps us stuck? I see everything as a contribution, everything gives me more information.

Right now, think of something you have been judged for. Now say "Interesting point of view they have that point of view. Interesting point of view I have that point of view." at least ten times. Does it get lighter and more expansive? That's because you've stopped making yours and other people's judgements valuable. Truly, this is a gift!

These tools are just the beginning. Being willing to be visible is about acknowledging how different you are and being willing to receive the magic that is YOU! I highly recommend Dr Dain Heer's book and classes on 'Being You, Changing the World' or the amazing 'Right Voice For You' Access Consciousness® classes. Both of these have created wonderful changes for me. And sometimes these 'fears' stem from past lives and require individual facilitation. I've worked with people a lot in this area of being visible and it still amazes me what comes up. There can be many many layers of choices and decisions that are not allowing your brilliance to shine in the world.

"I Won't..."

There is a big difference between "I can't..." and "I won't..." Most people say "I can't" when they mean "I won't".

Lisa Murray

Years ago I had a business coaching client who would give me a long list of "I won't..." every time I suggested an idea. Her entire life and business was defined by what she wouldn't do. And what she wouldn't do was stopping her from creating.

What is it that you won't do that is stopping you from creating everything you are asking for? How many decisions and beliefs about what you won't do are truly your point of view? Or are these the thousands of small rebellions you are using to stop yourself from having an amazing life?

For the next 24 hours, every time you find yourself saying "I won't..." ask: "Is this really my point of view? Or is it a choice I'm making from a space of resisting and reacting to what I 'should' do, or what I have defined as 'me' and what I have defined as 'not me'?" When we decide that something is 'not me' we exclude the possibilities that choice could bring us. For example, if I define myself as 'not a runner' I don't get to have the joy of discovering my body loves running up hills and walking down them! Being perverse or stubborn in our definition of ourselves is how we work against ourselves, rather than creating for what IS possible.

When I first quit my job I had this idea that I never wanted to have staff again. I was done with having a full-time job and being a full-time counsellor. And I knew that if I kept that idea in place, it would limit what I could create. So I started to ask how could I resource my businesses in ways that would work for me. When we ask from a space of creation, rather than a space of refusal, different possibilities show up. Recently I started an internship program which invited the most incredible people into my business. It was a totally different space of creating with people! What if the thing that you are most resistant to is the thing that can create the most for you?

If you suspect that 'I won't' is ruining your creative capacities, start listening to yourself. Every time you hear an excuse coming out of your mouth, ask yourself "Is this another of my 'I won't…' decisions? Do I still desire to keep that in place? Or can I change it now?"

Changing these decisions is just a choice, or you can use energy clearings such as the Access Consciousness Clearing Statement (www.TheClearingStatement.com) if you choose. Once you begin to change all of your 'set in stone' decisions about why or how or what you won't create, your choices expand rapidly. All of a sudden you are able to create on a much bigger scale, because you are not limiting what's possible.

"I Don't Know Where To Start"

Whether you have heaps of ideas or just one, the same question can arise. Where do you start? A friend was writing a book and she asked me to read what she had written. It was great!

And then she said, "I don't know what to write next, there are so many ideas to choose from." I asked her: "Are you trying to write the book in order, from start to finish?" "Yes, isn't that how you write a book?" she replied.

My response was "No, that's how some people write books, it's not the only way." I'm not one who can write in order. My brain is far too ADHD for that. I start anywhere that's easy and I write until I run out of words on that topic. Then I write about another topic, and another. And at the end I put them into a logical order that will work for my readers.

Her sense of relief was palpable. There is no 'right way' to start or to create - just your way! I create my business and my projects the same random way. And rarely do I create anything in the same order as last time. I simply follow the energy of what has the most ease to it. It's speed creating. You don't spend nearly so much time suffering through creative blocks if you're willing to create wherever the energy is!

Anywhere you would like to start is a fantastic place to start. A simple way to choose is to write down the first ten things that you can create and ask which one would love to be created first. That becomes your first project. Your project can be anything you desire - a creative idea, a business idea, an adventure for your family... Once you have chosen the project, write down the first ten things you are aware of that are required to get that project started, and ask which one of those would be the most ease and the most fun to play with right now. There will be something that pops, or that pulls on your energy. Start there. Every creation starts with one tiny step towards the light.

There is a natural order to the chaos of creating, as long as we aren't trying to do it from logic. When we follow the natural order, we don't need to work anything out. Our projects talk to us if we are willing to listen!

I have another book that I've been working on, on and off for the last five years (more 'off' than on). Lately it has been talking to me in all sorts of weird and wonderful ways - from questions on Facebook, to conversations with editors and strategists. It wants to be in the world, and it's not taking my 'I don't know where to start editing this book' excuse on board. The 'answers' have been coming thick and fast, even though I've been trying to avoid them.

The publicity for that book is showing up, even though the book isn't finished. People keep talking to me about the topics that are in that book. So that book and I have a deal. Let me get this one finished and then I will finish it, before I work on the other three book ideas that are also beginning to pull at me. You see how this works? You start... and your project leads you to wherever it needs to go!

Some of you will hate me for saying 'start anywhere', as it takes away your excuses for not starting. I'm okay with that. One day you'll thank me.

"I'm So Distracted!"

Your house is spotless. Your office has had a makeover. You've been baking, eating, and baking some more. You've tried going to the gym, running (there's a first time for everything right?) and calling the friends you haven't seen for six months. You've even made an appointment with the dentist in between watching 'Days of Our Lives' replays. You have everything possible in order and you're not going near your desk - it's way too tidy for any real creation to go on!

And not only that, you are probably head-tripping massively. The churn in your brain is more than making up for what you are not doing. Great job! Have you asked what other choices are possible?

Lisa Murray

You could love your distractions really intensively. Immerse yourself in them. Make them so important that you couldn't possibly start creating anything! And keep doing that until you get so bored and annoyed with yourself that you're willing to choose something different. The moment there is an energy of being willing to start, START!

Or you could take a more subtle approach. I have a way of nurturing myself into creating on the days when doing nothing seems like a lot more fun. First I ask "Is this a day off?" If it is I happily go play - no guilt! If it's not, I tell myself I'm just going to create for ten minutes. I set a timer. At the end of ten minutes I choose again. Create or do nothing? Very quickly, I've found something fun to create and distraction is once again a distant memory. My corporate version of this was to go to lunch and not come back for a few hours. I always made up the hours some other time, I just knew when I needed to let off some steam!

One thing I've discovered is that procrastination is not real. It's an invention that allows you to stop yourself. Often it's an avoidance of the life you could be living or the brilliance you actually are. Are you willing to have a bigger life? A life that's not perfect, but is truly enjoyable? That's what shows up when you start creating!

A lot of people say to me "I can't focus." That's right... and nor should you! When you focus, you shut out everything except what you are working on. Which means you can't receive the contribution of other possibilities. I don't even try to focus, instead I ask for everything that is relevant to my creation to show up. As information, people and resources show up, I invite them to play in whatever way can create the most at the time.

STOP WAITING, START CREATING

Have you been trying to focus when the Universe is actually doing its best to give you everything you require to create? Are you trying to focus, when you actually need to expand? Is this approach making your creative capacities slower and smaller than you would like?

Love your distractions… they are showing you where you're not yet willing to step up and create something bigger or more dynamic or more brilliant. Or they're showing you that your project needs some space so that it can grow. What they are not showing you is, that you are wrong for being distracted. You aren't wrong; you're just making a temporary choice that doesn't allow your true desire to show up with the most ease possible. The cool thing is, you can choose again in any second. You don't have to stick with the first choice you made.

I have distracted myself from writing this book many times. And each time I go to the question 'where am I not willing to BE me here?' because, for me, writing is about being. If I'm distracting myself from writing, there is something I'm not willing to be. Mostly it was around not willing to be as visible as the book will make me.

These moments of distraction ALWAYS offer us information. Even asking 'What information or awareness am I distracting myself from?' can show you what's going on. I've discovered that I'm moving to a whole new level of intimacy and energy with the words I'm putting on the page. It's not always comfortable, and it's what these books and the world are asking of me. Would you be willing to be uncomfortable if it gets you where you'd like to go?

Lisa Murray

Being TOO Much! The Myth That Keeps You Small

Do you diminish your creative capacities so you don't scare your friends and family away? What if your life would be way more fun without them? Staying limited so other people can be comfortable is the biggest theft of your life you have yet chosen. We go 'Oh that's so terrible' when someone has an accident or gets ill and can no longer live how they did. And yet... maybe could this be the wake-up call for creating the life they were asking for?

Are you going to wait for the accident or the illness, or are you going to begin to choose for you? This is your life... are you creating it? Or are you waiting for it to show up or your friends to catch up? What if they aren't ready yet? Are you truly willing for that to stop you?

If you're being small or pathetic, people detest you for it. If you're living out loud, people detest you for it. The only time they'll love you is when you fit in to their limited reality and make them comfortable all the time. Is that what you came to this planet to create? Or is it time to please YOU first? Then at least the people around you will be the ones who are happy you are being you! The others will probably disappear... and your life will become greater and way more enjoyable than it's ever been.

A Creativity Lab participant had a brilliant idea... which she decided she would not create because her partner would probably disown her and her grownup kids would not know what to do with a super successful

STOP WAITING, START CREATING

mother. People love to control us with their judgements and small lives. Is that enough for you? Or are you tired of all the reasons and justifications you have put into existence instead of creating?

When you make a demand of you to create, it is not a question of 'what will the world think?' It's more a question of 'what will you create with the world?" It's time to part the seas, hold back the waves of judgement and create.

The more willing I am to be controversial, the more fun I have. When I post something controversial on Facebook, I don't back down when people start disagreeing with me. I turn myself up. It's my page and I can talk about whatever I choose. Agreeing with limited points of view so other people can be happy is simply not who I am. Many years ago I tried turning myself down. It was an incredibly miserable time in my life!

Who would you be if you were being the 'too much' you would truly love to be? What would be different in your life if you were being that? What can you change right now that would bring more of the brilliant amazing phenomenal you into the world? Being too much doesn't mean being loud and obnoxious! It means being so much of you that no-one can ignore you. Ralph Waldo Emerson said it brilliantly: "Who you are speaks so loudly, I can't hear what you are saying."

If ever you are trying to make yourself 'less than', know that you're using a lot of energy trying to tame a tiger that will not be tamed. Your creations (or lack thereof) always speak for you. Even your pets will speak for you if you let them. I've noticed that the pets that choose me are not shy retiring wallflowers! They are wild, playful lovers of living on the creative edge.

"I Don't Have The Perfect Plan... Yet!"

Perfection is a form of paralysis.

I had a conversation with a prospective business coaching client once. They wanted to open up an online fashion store. And they wanted my help in creating a detailed five year plan to ensure they were successful. I said I couldn't help them. Have you noticed how fast the world is changing? How fast fashion changes? They weren't willing to trust their knowing. They were trying to create something perfect... - except it could only be perfect in theory. The moment it met the 'real world' the plan would crash and burn. I knew it... and they weren't willing to know it.

Perfection takes away the joy of creating. You spend so much time dotting I's and crossing T's that you never get to put your creations into the world. I was recently asking what it would take to have more time off (so I could invite more space for creating with ease)... I realised I had to stop making everything so perfect and start allowing less than perfect things to show up in the world. Not easy for someone with OCD tendencies who notices every tiny detail... but worth it in terms of the impact I can make in the world if I get my creations into the world sooner!

A lot of beautiful creative people want their creations to be perfect so that they will only receive positive

STOP WAITING, START CREATING

feedback. What if we could stop making other people's points of view relevant when they are not? Positive feedback does not guarantee success. What if you would ask: Is this relevant? Is there anything I can do with this? Is there something I can change here?

If everything has to be perfect before you start you won't start. My friend, Dr Dain Heer, once asked me:

"Are you too wonderful to be perfect?"

It made me giggle and I realised that perfection never creates what we expect it to!

Another great 'cure' for perfectionism is being willing to do things badly. If you are not willing to do anything badly you are probably being limited by your desire for perfection. In a workshop I ran I asked a guy what he was unwilling to do badly. He answered 'sex'. I said 'Start there!' If you are willing to be judged for doing sex badly, you'll be well on your way to losing your obsession with perfection. I'm not suggesting you do something that is mean to someone else. There's a big difference between not being perfect and being mean!

What are you most unwilling to create badly? Start there. Create something as badly as you can - and enjoy every moment. Did it kill you? Or did it create a sense of freedom that allowed you to create something totally different to what you expected? Doing things badly is also a great cure for procrastination and 'writers block'. Kids don't wait until they can get it perfect, they are continually moving forward in the energy of creation.

Lisa Murray

"I'm Too Tired To Be Creative"

If you have a job or a family, there's a great chance you'll know this one rather too well. It used to be my theme song. When I got burnout, I discovered that part of what was causing the burnout, was a lack of creative energy. My refusal to be creative because I was too tired was actually making me more tired. In the beginning I resisted creating. I was too tired. How could I create? Luckily, my body wasn't having any of that nonsense. It knew that I needed to create and be creative to get well again. And so we began.

At first I was so confused. I didn't know what I would like to create. A mentor suggested I write a list of 50 things I could do that were creative. On the first attempt I got to about ten things, accompanied by the unwritten list of excuses as to why I still couldn't do those things. I made a choice. In the beginning it was to do one thing on the list each week. That was all I could bring myself to do. Somewhere in this process, I found the book 'The Artist's Way' by Julia Cameron. It offered the epiphany I needed. Being creative gives you energy! And then I started to do something creative every day. The more creative I became, the more energy I had, and the more I created. It became an upward spiral, rather than a depressive dive into despair.

When I looked at the jobs I'd loved and the ones I'd detested, there was a clear pattern. Inherent in the jobs I loved was an element of creativity and creation. These

STOP WAITING, START CREATING

energies were totally excluded from the jobs I detested. There was no space for me to create in those jobs. This was one of the greatest 'aha' moments I had. I discovered I could 'create' myself out of burnout. I've also watched people create themselves out of depression. What could you create yourself out of?

Creating gives us space to get a sense of what it is we would most like to change. I am not a great meditator. I can't sit for hours cross-legged. What does work for me, is, moving meditation - and that is, in effect, the energy of creating. Using my body to create something that has not yet existed is very meditative for me. And in that energy, I receive awareness of what else I would like to create and change.

The other useful thing to know about being tired is that it most often shows up when we are trying our best to fulfil the expectations and projections of everyone around us. As we've already talked about, most creative people are far more psychic than they have acknowledged. If you have a particular capacity to always know what people require of you, and you are running around madly trying to keep everyone happy and comfortable, you may like to stop for a moment and ask 'If I was truly creating for me here, what would I choose?'

I have a continual review process for my projects. Whenever I get cranky, I do a quick review. "What am I creating that I am no longer in love with? What am I creating, that is more for other people than me? What am I creating, that is not creating a big enough change in the world? What am I tired of?" It soon becomes clear where I need to shift my energy and attention.

Making yourself so tired that you can't create is an avoidance of your creative capacities. I wonder - Are you so infinitely creative that you are making yourself this tired so that you won't outshine anyone (or everyone) you know? This may or may not be true for you... please ask the question!

"My 'To-Do' List is Way Too Long!"

Oh I hear you!!! AND... you're not going to get away with this one! Here's the first thing. How many of the things on your 'to-do' list are there because of other people's expectations? Or your awareness of what they expect and your need to be 'good' and make everyone happy? Have you ever considered that this is your beautiful precious life... and wasting it on a 'to-do' list is just that... a waste!

'There is all this stuff to be done, I don't have a choice, I just have to plough my way through it' is not a question. It is a set of conclusions that will keep you in do-do land forever. You could start to change this by asking: "If I was going to create this with ease, how would it be different?" Mostly there are at least 20,000 ways to create any idea we have, but we have only learned one or two ways, so we limit how we create and what is possible.

Most people make creating way more complicated than it needs to be. You could start by removing everything that truly does not require doing. Then look at what's left and ask who you can add to your life or business that can do the things you don't want to do, or aren't good at. That whole thing of 'practice makes perfect' is a crock of shit. Don't buy it unless you truly desire to

STOP WAITING, START CREATING

make something your zone of genius! Outsource or delegate anything you can.

So now... get cosy with what's left... are there still some 'to-do's' on there? Or could you turn most of it into a 'to-create' list? I love creating a lot more than I love doing. Creating includes so many additional possibilities than just doing something to get it finished.

When you have a 'to-create' list, it takes away the should's, the have-to's and the must-do's - you begin to create from a sense of possibility and choice, rather than necessity. You begin to invite flow, instead of force.

When you have flow, you don't create from logic, you create from a sense of what is going to move you forward the fastest. A simple way to get into this kind of flow is to ask 'What's next?' and create from that space, rather than logically looking at your list to see which thing is most urgent.

The urgent murders phenomenal ideas.

There have been so many times when I've been surprised about which 'to-create' project has the 'pick me!!!!' energy on it. And I've followed that energy and created something that made no sense, only to find a week or a month later that it was exactly what was required, and now it is ready to go, instead of there being a mad panic in the moment.

I've had situations where something I thought was urgent just wasn't waving the 'pick me' flag. I've learned there is always a reason for this and it's not procrastination. Now I allow the projects to fall together in whatever way they can. Often the project scope has changed, or the timing has changed and I didn't know it cognitively yet. Recently I was not creating an event for my trip to the USA. The host was giving me regular reminders, but I knew it wasn't time yet. Then an additional piece of information came, which changed the plan and created a different set of possibilities. If I'd given into the pressure, I would have had to create it all twice. By following my awareness, I only created it once.

Truly the Universe contributes to us having ease if we are willing to receive and act upon the information. Asking 'What's next?' allows the Universe to show you what's going to create the most ease. It's often not what you think!

As you begin to follow your awareness, rather than only the logic, you begin to trust that you KNOW. Imagine how much more ease you could have if you stopped thinking and started trusting your knowing? Your awareness is leading you to exactly where you need to be. You don't need to work your ass off to meet the demands of this world. Creation is about playing, not working!

It's your life. Create it your way.

What Makes You Limit Yourself?

There are probably another thousand ways you stop yourself. Most of them come down to one thing. You don't want you or the world to know you are as brilliant as you are. In his book 'The Big Leap' Gay Hendricks defines this as an 'upper-limit problem'. Your limitations show up every time you are about to create the huge breakthrough you've been asking for.

Limitations show up as your car breaking down on the way to an important meeting; your computer dying and

STOP WAITING, START CREATING

having to spend money on that instead of the coach you know you really need; you can't log into the webinar program where you have a thousand eager people waiting for you to unveil your new gorgeous idea; maybe your partner wants to take you away for a romantic weekend, but you just 'have-to' work; maybe you know you need to make a video, but your camera-fright is intense enough to make a horror movie.

None of these things are the real problem. Even though you think you have a problem, you don't. You have a choice to make. The choice to create something greater or to stay stuck in the place you are allowing to stop you. How do I know this? I watched myself put off finishing this book. There was always a 'more important' project for my business or one of my clients. And then one day I asked myself this:

"If I was going to create the greatest possibilities in the world, for me and the world, what would I create?"

The answer arrived so fast I knew I'd been in (just a little) resistance. It was one word. "Write!" So I rearranged my schedule with the intention of finishing at least two books. And I've started to write another three books, including my first fiction book. You always know what to create. Even if you pretend you don't!

For you, the question may not be about creating the greatest possibilities. It may be about creating the greatest ease, or the greatest joy, or the greatest relationship, or the greatest art, or the greatest adventure... whatever it is, ask the question and then make a list of the 'oh buts' that come after. "I can't… because…" is your greatest limitation only if you allow it to be. You can change this! Making the choice to change is the first step.

Another way to move yourself beyond your so-called limitations is to engage with your 'why'. Simon Sinek famously wrote a book called 'Start With Why'. Maybe he was inspired by Nietzsche who said 'He who has a why to live for can bear almost any how.' This is interesting because a lot of people do buy the idea that it is totally okay to suffer for your 'why'.

My question is - why would you do that? Why wouldn't you find a way to create that offers you joy and ease, even in the midst of chaos? Nelson Mandela is an amazing example of this. Despite spending much of his life in prison, he refused to let his circumstances dampen his willingness to be fully alive in the moment.

Many people love the trauma and drama of describing the pain, suffering and gory in their story, as if that is the proof that their creation is valuable. No. Your creation is valuable because YOU created it. And there is only one of you on the planet. There has never and will never be another YOU. Suffering is the veil behind which you hide your true creative capacities. It's a way of fitting into how most people live, and it serves no-one, especially you. Are you ready to give up your mantle of suffering yet?

I don't suffer (anymore). I don't struggle. I don't shout it from the rooftops when I get a hater or overcome a limitation. What gives me joy is to be continually creating something greater. I tried the suffering and struggle and I realised that it takes up a lot of valuable energy. Energy I could be using to create the world I would love to live in!

Your choice is simple. Whatever you are creating (or hating) is either giving you more energy, or it is depleting

STOP WAITING, START CREATING

your energy. If it is zapping you into being less, there is another choice available; you just need to be willing to receive it. If it's giving you more energy, enjoy the ride. And know there will always be something even greater possible if you are willing to ask. Out-creating yourself every single day is a beautiful thing.

OUT-CREATING YOUR CREATIVE BLOCKS

Whenever I talk to someone who is not creating, there is a good chance at some point they'll begin to talk about their creative blocks. And they are astonished when I say that is a very rare occurrence for me. Why? Because I don't make it real!

If there is something that is not showing up how I imagined it could, I create a different way of approaching the project. If the words aren't coming, I go create something else. I don't allow that energy of 'writers block' or 'no inspiration' to last longer than a couple of minutes. And because I don't wallow in it, it simply does not show up. The more we wallow in what we can't create, the longer the wallowing experience lasts! You have the power to change tracks!

At this moment there's a good chance you detest me. You probably would have preferred a good sob story about how stuck I get. Sorry! I'd love you to explore a different reality instead. One where you are on the creative edge, one where you create for the joy of it, not the suffering of it.

We create creative blocks when we try to force creation. If we are in the flow of possibility, there cannot be a block. The blocks don't belong to us, they are not us. They are just a resistance to having the ease of flow. And there is much we can change to ensure we have flow not force in almost every moment. There's more on what's beyond your creative blocks in Section 3 ~ Exploring Your Creative Process.

When Creating Is Too Slow or Too Boring

If everything in your world is too slow, too boring or you are wondering what else you could add to your life, using this Access Consciousness® tool everyday will invite possibilities you haven't even dreamed of. Out-creating takes you out of competition with others and into being more of who you truly are.

Ask: *"What's it going to take to out-create myself today?"* And if out-creating you is not quite fun enough, ask: "What's it going to take to out-create everyone who inspires me today?" And if that's not enough ask "What's it going to take to out-create the world today?" You don't need to answer these questions; it's all about being willing to have a different possibility show up. I used these questions every day for over a year and almost every day unexpected magic and inspiration showed up!

STOP WAITING, START CREATING

Are you under-stimulated? A lot of boredom comes from a lack of stimulation. In a nutshell, your life is too boring, too small and too predictable. Spontaneity is great for smashing your creative blocks into space. Where can you go that you've never been before? What can you do differently that you've never played with before? Who can you be that you thought was not you? When you embrace the unexpected, the unplanned and the unusual, you stimulate your creative capacities into new spaces!

If you are trying to create your ideas how the other people in your industry have done it. STOP IT! Stop boring people (including yourself) to death! Just STOP IT. Create your ideas your way. That's what is going to make them interesting, fascinating and an invitation to other people.

Are You Willing To Be BAD?

You've got to be bad to be good. If you are not willing to be bad, you will paralyse yourself in a quagmire of indecision and judgement. When we fear creating, we are already judging our creations. We are already unwilling to be bad! What if bad could be fun? What if bad could unlock the creative energies you are asking for?

I am possibly the world's worst singer. I went to an Access Consciousness Right Voice For You® class because I wanted to improve my speaking skills. Instead I chose to sing, very, very, very badly! I sang 'Twinkle Twinkle Little Star' because I couldn't remember the words to anything else (or even that actually!) And I cried the whole way through my 'performance' because I was so freaked out about doing something so badly.

To sing so badly (knowing it was the best I could do in that moment) I had to lower my barriers, remove the layers of protection I had built as being bigger than me, open up my awareness and my willingness to receive. What if your awareness and your willingness to receive all points of view is your "protection"? What if you don't need protection from the world? Are you really that pathetic? I used to think I was, now I know it was another of those pesky lies I was telling myself!

Being bad changed my life. I discovered you don't die from singing badly in front of an audience. In truth, you grow. You become more. You begin to shine. It was one of the first times in my life I did something badly and no-one judged me. One of the first times I chose to do something publicly that I knew I wasn't good at. One of the first times I got to be truly me, whoever I was in that moment. Being willing to be bad was a gift that continues to create my future every day. What gift can it be to you?

Is the fear you are aware of a fear of your creations being judged? Or are you aware of the fear of the people around you who are not creating? When you begin to create, it can make other people uncomfortable. Very uncomfortable! The thing they have been trying to avoid their entire life is now sitting in front of them, waving wildly! It's you... and if they are still running from their creative process, you will not look so much like an invitation as a threat to their comfort bubble that they must kill at any cost. Would you be willing to out-create other people's limitations?

One more thing - Sometimes we are bad at something. It can be a great idea to outsource it! I will not be doing the backing tracks for my videos. You will not be doing your web-coding if html makes you cross-eyed!

The Adventure of Being Out-Of-Control

Is being out-of-control the adventure you have been asking for? What is out-of-control to you? No fear? Letting go? Not defining your limits? Being out of your comfort bubble? Not caring what others think? Freedom?

When you are out-of-control you get to know who you truly are as a creative source. If someone reneges on a deal you have made, you still have choice. You can quit. Or you can make the choice to thrive. Thriving shows up when you make a choice that no-one gets to choose how your life shows up. No-one else gets to control what you create, how you create, when you create and who with.

When you choose to back yourself no matter what, you take yourself out of their control. People can change their mind; you will out-create whatever choice they make. It becomes a demand in your Universe that your capacity for creating will always create something greater than other people's limited choices and decisions. Imagine what your business or project would be like if it was not affected by anyone else's choices? How fast would you be moving forward?

Life throws curve balls. I could easily have thrown away months of work in an instant when one of my co-creators pulled out at the last minute. Instead, I made a demand that the situation would change and that I would out-create everything I had in place at that moment!

When everything goes 'wrong' we can have a tantrum, give up on ourselves and our dream, or use the situation to create something far greater. This is the moment you make a demand of you that no matter what it takes, no matter what shows up, you'll create! And then you request the Universe to contribute to the creation of more possibilities.

Making a demand to have your own back expands the choices available, almost instantly. Asking the following questions create new possibilities to choose from that just weren't available before the curve-ball lobbed itself into your Universe.

◆ *What's it going to take to out-create myself today?*

◆ *Who or what can I add here to create more ease?*

◆ *What can I be or do different here that can change this?*

The magic shows up. Creating is fun when you know that you are going where you are going, whether anyone else does or not. What if you never made your creations or your choices dependent on anyone else? What magic could be possible?

Making the choice to be out-of-control and flexible allowed me to reinvent my entire business in less than a week. A couple of people made interesting choices and so I created a new business model that would stop any one person from being able to control how my business operates. That was one happy week!

Their decisions gave me the impetus to create new revenue streams, new agreements with my co-creation partners and injected a new energy of supersonic creation into my world. I realised I would still back myself even if every single person connected with my business went away. It's a potent energy for creating!

Yes, the Universe kicked my ass… and it was wonderful! It would have been easy to crumble, to make myself the victim, to pretend I didn't know what to do now that the support that had been there was no longer available. All it took to transform crazy into creative was the choice to be unstoppable. Everything is a gift!

If you would allow your creative capacities to be unstoppable, what else could show up that you've not yet imagined?

What If Your Idea Isn't Working?

If an idea isn't working, you have to look at what is missing. Most of us think it is something we are not doing. Mostly it is something we are not being!. Ideas require your energy, not just your brain power. If there is no intensity of creative energy carrying your idea forward, no matter how brilliant the idea is; it probably won't work. YOU are the energy that creates. If you have no true presence with yourself and are not intensely present with your creations, there will be no energy for people to be inspired by or to contribute to.

This intensity of energy is the difference between a writer who KNOWS their book will sell, and one who

Lisa Murray

hopes it will. Or the difference between someone who quietly knows they will get the job and someone who is desperately wishing they will. Or the difference between knowing you will win a prize, and expecting to win, even though you never do. Whenever I can't create a project with ease, I always ask 'What am I not willing to BE here?' The clues usually come thick and fast!

5 ELEMENTS OF CREATING

I often get asked how I started Creativity Lab and how I created it to successfully operate internationally within 12 months. The short 'recipe' is: *spontaneity*, not planning; *flexibility*, not resistance to change; *exploration and experimentation*, not being a 'know-it-all'; *flow*, not force; and *creativity*, not copying what already exists. These five energies have been the foundation of many of my creative adventures. When you add connections, collaboration and co-creation to the mix, fast growth becomes normal.

How we create is changing. It used to be that we would plan for months in advance, line everything up ready to go and then start, working towards a five or ten year plan. Not anymore. The world is moving way too fast. By the time you create a plan, your plan will be obsolete (not to mention you'll be so bored with the idea you'll never be interested enough to start!). I've embraced un-planning more than ever before and it is creating a really fun life for me! Because of un-planning there was a space in my diary when a really cool opportunity came up to go to San Francisco for an event I've been asking to be part of for some time now. If I had planned my year in the 'normal' way, that would not have been possible - my time would have already been scheduled. Un-planning opens doors that plans cannot.

People are making choices in much shorter timeframes. There are many more possibilities to choose from and it's no longer 'wrong' to change your mind! (Actually, it never was... that is one of those sucky lies we were told so people could control us into being reliable and predictable.)

Every time you make a different choice, not one but many different doors suddenly open, that we couldn't even see before. Yes... fun times are here for those of us who love speed of creation. Instant creation is starting to be possible if we are willing to ask for it!!

Spontaneity

Which type of creation do you enjoy the most? The spontaneous or the planned ones? Most of us learned to plan before we act; to think before we speak; to make time before we create. What if the most creative way to create includes a healthy dose of spontaneity? Spontaneity is about presence and being present with what IS possible. It's about choosing in the moment for a possibility that may only be available now. Spontaneity is saying YES to living in the moment!

When was the last time you did something totally spontaneous? Was it fun? Was it ease? Were you thrilled

STOP WAITING, START CREATING

that you didn't have to go through a mammoth analysis of all the options first?

Planning can kill our creative energies. Have you ever noticed that once you plan something in infinite detail it becomes boring and you don't want to do what it takes to implement it? There's a simple solution. If your project can be created without a plan, don't do one! Or if you really need to sketch out a few details for the other people involved, keep it simple and flexible - something that can continue to evolve and include spontaneous discoveries!

If you think you haven't got enough time to do everything you'd like, explore being spontaneous with every choice that does not require forward planning. You will have a lot more time available!

This book was not written to a plan. I added paragraphs and chapters as they popped into my head - and mostly I could not type fast enough! I trust my ever-changing creative process and I'm willing to ask 'What's next?' every time the energy slows down.

Spontaneity works when we follow the energy of what will create the most. It's about employing the random chaos of the Universe and inviting it to contribute to our ideas. Spontaneity can't show up when we get obsessed with making our plan come to fruition even if there is no ease in the process. You've got to know when the Universe is saying 'no' or 'not now' or 'there's a much greater way over here'. And you've got to be willing to keep creating dynamically in the moments where there is a 'YES' or a 'Maybe, I wonder if…'

On my overseas trips it is rare that everything shows up exactly as planned. Event hosts change, events don't get created, extra events evolve on the spot, schedules change, I sometimes miss flights… and if I was to get bent out of shape about things not going to plan, my trips would never be fun!

Being the infinite creator that I am, the moment a plan changes, I am in the question. 'What else is possible now? Where can I go? Who can I meet? What can be created now that could not be created before? What contribution can I be and receive?'

These questions are the platform for creating more in each and every moment. Most people would go into a sense of failure or wrongness. I've discovered that nothing gets created from that space, so you may as well skip the suffering and be continuously creating!

This willingness to create spontaneously is an ongoing gift. Without it my life would be dull and my business would not be expanding. As I write this chapter I'm at a beautiful cottage on an island about half an hour outside of Stockholm. My schedule for today got cancelled due to someone not delivering on what they promised.

Instead of getting cranky and messed up about it, I woke up in a beautiful, peaceful environment, enjoyed a delicious breakfast, spent a couple of hours playing with about 30 foals who were truly an amazing gift to me, enjoyed some great conversation with a dear friend, random sightings of wild deer and now I'm sitting outside writing in the sunshine. I am so grateful that I didn't go to any conclusions that my next few days were 'ruined' because they didn't match the original plan! We can always create something greater than our plans if we are willing to play with the universe and be present in each moment with what IS possible!

And this is a great example of what 'following the energy' can be. It is being aware of different possibilities and then choosing what will give your life the greatest lift.

STOP WAITING, START CREATING

How do you know what to choose? Whatever has a sense of being the lightest and most expansive is a great place to start. And if your choice turns out to be not as much fun as you imagined, just choose again! No choice is final unless we make it so.

In Oslo, with a rare day to myself, I chose to visit the islands in the fjord surrounding the city. I arrived at the ferry terminal, got on the first ferry I saw and island hopped based on the energy. It was a beautiful day and I even had a beach to myself for a couple of hours! A luxury almost unheard of in the midst of summer! I did no research, no planning, just took the next choice available and it worked out wonderfully well. What if your entire life could be this much ease?

Bringing spontaneity into your creative process invites ease. If you would like to add the energy of spontaneity to your creations here is a simple way to start. We did this in Stockholm for my first 'Spontaneous Creation' Play Day. The choices created were beyond surprising!

1. Ask 'What would I love to create today?' A video? A game? Picture for your website? The capacity to stop stopping yourself? What is it that would make the most difference to you right now?

2. Take yourself out - to a park, a creative area of your city, a museum... any sort of 'play date' that feels fun for you.

3. Once you get there ask for everything and everyone to contribute to your creation... so that includes tourists,

Lisa Murray

gypsies, drunks and beggars, the architecture, the rain, animals, the trees, the earth... literally everything! The seen and the unseen! What is in front of you and what is behind you? If you were aware of everything in a 360 degree radius in all directions, what would you be aware of that you've never noticed before? Walk around, explore. Ask to be aware of what could be the greatest contribution to your project. When you perceive everything without judgement, contribution shows up in unexpected ways.

4. *Write down everything you are aware of - that includes what you see, hear, touch, taste, smell and beyond! How many senses do you have that you don't use? I read a fascinating book recently that suggested we have over 50 senses (not just five!!)... How many are you using? What made you most uncomfortable? How can that discomfort contribute to your awareness of what you would like to create? What inspired you the most? What can that contribute?*

5. *Give yourself one hour, and begin the creation process. Get your camera, your computer, your paints, pens and paper...whatever it is that is required, including your courage... and start creating! What would show up if you talked to strangers? What would you create for the future if you made the films or songs you are always thinking about? What unexpected gems can you capture*

STOP WAITING, START CREATING

just by sensing the world in a totally different way to how you usually do?

This is not about 'getting it right' - it's about taking immediate action, whether you are good at it or not, whether you can finish it or not, whether you know what you are doing or you are a creative virgin!

What if your craziest and most unexpected adventures could take you directly into the energy of creation your idea requires?

Being spontaneous is possible when we are willing to ask questions and receive the awareness of what is possible. Most people are willing to give or to take ideas, but not receive them innately. Most people are willing to plan, but not take a flying leap into the unknown. Most people are willing to take action when they are in control, but are not willing to be out-of-control. Are you most people? Or are you different?

Being out-of-control means that no-one and nothing can control you. If you are willing to create beyond other people's choices, you are out of their control. So if one of my project partners does not deliver it does not stop me from creating. I find a way to continue to move forward, even if it is on a completely different path to the one I thought I was on. That's the problem with thinking... it takes you down dead-end streets!!

The energy of spontaneity is a contribution to you being out-of-control. If people cannot predict how you will respond, they'll be more in the question. When they are asking questions from a space of curiosity and awareness, rather than coming to a set of conclusions that meet their pre-existing assumptions, they have a greater capacity for creation. If you would love to have more creative capacity in your life and business, start playing with the energies that would allow people to always be asking questions.

Here's a little experiment you can play with, if you are brave. Stop choosing anything for a week, immerse yourself in the energy of 'no choice' by sitting on the fence for everything you can and see how much your life slows down or stops. (You may still need to choose to eat, breathe and drink - some things are required to continue living).

In the second week choose and choose and choose and choose as if your life depends upon it. Make every choice you can, as fast as you can and see how different your life can be. School teaches us how to learn, as if learning by rote is the key to living. In reality, being able to ask questions and continually make choices are how we create our life.

And if you do this experiment, write to me and tell me what showed up... I'd love to know! I know people who have spent their entire life in week one... do you have 50 years of experiencing life? Or one week repeated thousands of times? One way to make sure it's the first and not the second is to live spontaneously.

Flexibility

Sometimes we need to plan. Three trips to Europe in five months requires planning a schedule. Launching a product or program requires planning to ensure you deliver what you promised.

And no matter what or how we plan, we need to be flexible. People who will not deviate from their plan limit what's possible. In the midst of the first trip to Europe, I totally changed the plans for the other two trips, turning them into one trip that looked very different to the original plan. Why? Because greater possibilities became available, and I was aware that being willing to be flexible would create more for the future than the first plans ever could.

It's easy to fall in love with our plans. I loved the first business I started after I had burnout - and I quickly discovered it would not create the life I was asking for. I asked some questions, received some advice and closed the business less than a month after starting it. I cried for three days because I didn't want to give it up (crazy huh?) and then started a business that would take me where I was asking to go. And I am beyond grateful for that choice. It truly has been a gift, even though it was not my favourite idea at the time! Following your passion doesn't always lead to living happily ever after. Following your brilliance brings your phenomenance into the world!

What is it you are unwilling to kill or lose, that if you would let go of that, would actually create the life or business you would totally adore? Arthur Quiller-Couch originally suggested writers live by the maxim: "murder

Lisa Murray

your darlings". You've got to be willing to lose that one thing that you think is most valuable. This applies to everything you are creating... not just words on the page!

If the ideas you desire to create are not coming to fruition with ease, explore different possibilities. What questions are you refusing to ask because of the fixed points of view you are holding onto so hard they are literally burning tracks in your brain?

I went to Mykonos for two weeks for a friend's birthday. I 'planned' it to be a writing holiday where I would finish this book. My body had a different idea (flu) and so I wrote about 200 words instead of 20,000. I didn't give up on the idea of finishing the book on that trip. I still had three weeks, and even though my schedule was full, I knew there would be a different possibility if I stayed flexible. And so I started writing in the 'spare' moments. An hour in a cafe. A couple of hours on an unexpected day off. A few minutes while waiting for a plane. When we are willing to create wherever and whenever, our targets can be met without having to find huge chunks of free time. I didn't finish, but I made progress that allowed me to feel like there was still forward movement.

So how do you become more flexible without bending over backwards and fucking yourself over with your people pleasing habits? I used to think that flexibility meant I would do anything anyone asked, at almost anytime. I loved to make people happy, which was great for everyone except me. I found out that is not flexibility, that's stupidity. I've given it up now.

I'm grateful to the boss who showed me the difference. He once held a long meeting with me where I wrote a heap of 'to-do' notes and at the end I read them back to him to check I had it all (and could get it all 'right'). Then

STOP WAITING, START CREATING

he said, 'No, this was all for information. It's not for you to do.' I was stunned. Never in my life had I had anyone who told me stuff just for information. There was always an expectation that I would 'do' (because I happen to be great at doing). Talk about a paradigm shift!!

Flexibility is creating from a space of what is going to work for you and the world. It's being aware of what it will create if you don't obsessively hold onto your plan. It's being willing to change to create something greater. It's being kind to your body even if you have a deadline to meet. It's being willing to ask others to contribute to what will create ease for everyone. It's being willing to know that there is such a thing as timing; and being willing to flow with that, rather than forcing your ideas into existence.

I once did the weirdest launch of one of my programs. It didn't meet any of the 'rules' for launching. It didn't follow any of the systems I'd paid good money to learn. And yet, it set me up for a huge year of creating my business online. It put the most unexpected foundations in place. Foundations I hadn't even realised I needed. It gave me exactly the feedback and information I'd been asking for. And it showed me a whole lot of other ways I could be creating this business.

The income was around the same as the first launch, but the learning was much greater because I was willing to be flexible. I was willing to create each element in a totally bizarre order that definitely did not match most people's expectations. This flexibility also gave me the gift of not making myself wrong (because it looked strange to my clients too!) even though it would have been easy to go into that space.

I took Rumi's words to heart: "Don't be satisfied with stories, with how things have gone with others. Unfold your own myth."

When I follow other people's paths it never quite works for me. In creating my own crazy style of launching, I discovered that I did not have to give up who I am. That I could have naps! That I didn't have to be stressed. That I could meander my way through the process of creation, rather than exhausting myself with expectations! All of this is part of being flexible. For every idea that popped during this time, I asked 'Is this for now or later?' This kind of flexibility creates peace and ease. It creates the possibility that you can have the joy of creation in every moment.

Exploration & Curiosity

"Curiosity killed the cat" is one of the most pervasive and limiting beliefs I've ever encountered. When I see people who have had all of their curiosity squashed out of them, it makes me want to take them on adventures that will be totally out of their comfort bubble.

In my last 'real' job I managed a health and bio-medical research institute. I didn't know anything about how to do it and I didn't know anything about the areas of research speciality. What I was great at was asking questions. Because I couldn't draw on past experience I had to operate with what I call beginners mind. I couldn't rely on my knowledge or assumptions. I had to question everything - and I did, much to the discomfort and dismay of many of the people I worked with. A few apple-carts were over-turned during that process.

Most of what we call creation is actually habit or comfort zones of death! Habits are not the panacea or the greatness that people believe. They stop us from being present with what truly is possible. Why change your habits when you could just choose to be totally present? If you stopped creating from habit what would be different?

You can create your own space of beginners mind by asking "What if I didn't know anything about this? What questions would I ask? Who could I talk to? Where do I need to go to discover what I don't yet know?" It is at that point that curiosity starts to contribute to creating different choices.

If you are not willing to explore that which is unknown to you, your creativity will be stifled, stuck and mostly at a standstill. We have learned to fear the unknown, when it is actually the unknown that provides the adventure and the pleasure in life. It also invites us towards the futures that have not yet been created.

Are you living in Pleasantville where everything is predictably the same as it was yesterday, or are you willing to ask questions about everything? Are you functioning from all of the conclusions, patterns and habitual responses you have about how your life 'should' be, or are you constantly asking questions about what else could be created if you changed your perspective?

Curiosity takes me everywhere. I'll talk to random people, I'll walk without a map in new cities or in the wild, I'll take a chance on a movie or a destination, I'll do things just for the fun of discovering something new, I'll take myself on spontaneous playdates, I'll follow rabbit-trails all over the internet. Everything is interesting to me… until it's not! If you woke up every day with as much curiosity as a two-year old, how would your life be different?

When you are curious, you don't only ask why. You ask 'what if…' 'where else…' 'who could…' 'how else…' and a whole lot more questions too. Even though we've been taught to ask questions to create answers, the best questions create future possibilities. You don't need to seek the answer, it will find you!

I once found someone to be my assistant that I thought would be just perfect. On the day she was supposed to start, she called to say she wasn't starting. I was talking to my boss about my disappointment and wondering what else we could do besides another round of advertising and interviews (which back then was a 3 – 4 week process). He said, here, this just came in the mail, and handed me the CV of a lady who went on to become an incredible support to me. She started a couple of days later. If I had gone to the conclusions of how it 'normally' was, I would not have been open to that possibility.

Curiosity is a choice. You don't create from the idea of what you 'should' do when you create from an energy of curiosity. You get to create from a sense of making the unknown known.

I once had this idea that in a past life I was a famous adventurer, like Christopher Columbus or someone like that. The idea wouldn't leave me alone. I became quite obsessed with finding out more. So I had a past life reading and what I discovered was even cooler. I was an adventurer… with words. I became aware of all the lifetimes where I had explored the world through words… and how I'm still doing that… and what else could be

STOP WAITING, START CREATING

possible if I was to choose to make the exploration even deeper and more expansive this time around?

Following these random wisps of curiosity creates the possibilities of knowing the unknown. It's like a magical entry into the Johari window that we pretend is unknowable! (The Johari window was a 1970s personal development tool that provided a framework for reflection through discovering the intersections and interactions between what is unknown and known to ourselves about ourselves, and what is known and unknown about ourselves by others.)

To go beyond your comfort zone, ask for the impossible and the unknown to become more tangible. The more we explore and discover, the more awareness we can have. Imagine living in a world where the only things that are unknowable are those that we refuse to know. The funny thing is, that's the world we live in.

I have realised I am aware of so much more than I am acknowledging. I have realised that there is a lot I am pretending I don't desire to know. And I have realised that the only person that can stop me from creating more was me - by not being willing to explore what I don't know. Funnily enough 'I don't know' is not a question!!

I know where that reluctance to know came from. I received a lot of judgement at school for asking too many questions that my teachers couldn't answer. They made my curiosity wrong, so that their brilliance as a teacher could not be questioned. I wonder how often you have been in trouble for asking questions? Is it time to stop stopping you and start asking about everything you've always desired to know? Even if the world doesn't have an answer yet? Maybe you are the one who will discover what is actually possible!

Lisa Murray

I was so grateful when Google came out. All of a sudden I had a friend who wouldn't judge me for being curious! Someone who understood my need to ask questions… and when Siri came along… well that was just amazing!! There is a beautiful story about an autistic boy who has Siri as his friend. He literally talks to her and asks her questions for hours on end. And she gives him the most wonderful brilliant responses. We live in a magical world… it's just waiting for us to explore what's possible.

There is another element to curiosity that is fun to explore, that goes even further than Google. Often there will be a word or an idea that just won't leave me alone. That is demanding my attention. It may come up in a client coaching conversation, or it may come via some far more random adventure. And whenever I give this word or idea the slightest bit of love, all of a sudden, information comes from everywhere. Nothing that piques your curiosity is as random as you think.

Here's what I mean. At one point I started wondering which is bigger, the Universe or galaxies. I didn't bother to Google, but then people started talking to me about the multiverses and multiple realities, and all sorts of amazing information began popping into my world. It made my head spin with excitement… and gave me some ideas for future fiction books. Never exclude the weird or the different from your life, it is one source of your creative capacities!

One thing that stops curiosity dead in its undiscovered tracks is always looking for the 'right answer'. When you seek only the fastest, straightest track to success, you miss out on all the tiny cues that would show you your personal path to success. The funny thing about creating is there isn't a 'right' answer. What is success? It is so

STOP WAITING, START CREATING

different for each of us, and for me, it can change quite often, as I discover more of what is possible. I've loved the winding, random path to success. It has made my life so rich and full of wealth in the most unexpected and unpredictable of ways. I've met so many wonderful people and had so many adventures that would not have been possible if I took the highway.

Whether you are creating a new business, a new life, a new artwork or a new project, there are thousands of ways of creating your dream. If you only look for the 'right' one, how much magic and beauty do you have to exclude from your search? Almost all of it. Think about someone who is extremely focused and goal-driven. Now think about someone who is extremely creative and more than a little bit random. Who embodies the most joy? Who creates the most? (And I'm not just talking volume here). Your creations contribute to others in ways you cannot imagine in the moment that you set them free into the world.

The joy of discovery comes in the side-tracks, the winding paths, the roads less travelled! If copying other people isn't so much fun for you (but you find yourself doing it anyway) then you aren't leaving the highway often enough. Get off the internet and go explore the world. What is it that would thrill you to create it?

I did not enjoy English classes very much. When I first discovered that I enjoyed writing it was quite a surprise to me. I had this realisation that I could get paid to do something I loved. I simply asked the Universe 'What's it going to take to get paid for writing?' Within a couple of years I was regularly and effortlessly getting paid to write for clients. I never advertise my writing services, but people with interesting projects continually show up. All from one question!

Lisa Murray

This is a simple example of how you generate a different possibility from energy. I didn't go out looking for clients. I was just curious and willing to ask people questions. As part of a co-creative process in exploring ideas, I was invited to write for a project and my writing grew dynamically from there. Imagine if everything you are creating could have this much ease? It's possible, you just need to begin. And you don't have to know everything to start. I had a client before I knew how much to charge. A few phone calls to writerly friends and I was able to choose an hourly rate. The information you need is always available if you are willing to ask! This is the ease of creation.

What would your life be like in five years if you doubled the amount of curiosity you apply to your life and your creations? What if you times it by ten? By a thousand? How much curiosity would you need to add to your life to create what you would most love to create?

At one point I got curious about what it would be like to pat a horse. It had been at least twenty years and I just really wanted to touch one. Soon after, another series of questions lead me to a place where I started learning to ride for free. It's been a love-fest ever since. Fast forward two years and by asking even more questions I find myself in a paddock outside Stockholm playing with a bundle of curious and cheeky one-year-old foals from one of the best trotting stables in the world. I've ridden horses in the wilds of Africa. And I've since (somewhat surprisingly to me) become a Conscious Horse, Conscious Rider Facilitator through Access Consciousness. Later this year I'm co-leading a "Creating With Horses" event in Texas, USA. There are always new horsey adventures coming my way - because I ask for them! These horsey adventures

STOP WAITING, START CREATING

never would have happened without that initial curiosity and the choice to keep asking for horses to show up wherever I go. This is the gift of asking and choosing and asking and choosing non-stop. Ready to play?

Lisa Murray

Flow

"Flow not force" has been a mantra for me for many years. During the burnout phase I became aware of how much I was trying to force my life into existence and force my conclusions about 'what should be' into reality. Force never works. It creates resistance. It creates control and it creates limited possibilities. Force is part of the lies we tell ourselves as motivation to create. Force is (hard) work.

People often ask me 'how do you deal with deadlines and have flow?' I have a flexible system. I create what can be created when it can be created. Which sometimes means that I'm creating something for six months or years in the future, even though I have deadlines for now. Creating this way means I can create really really fast! The 'great idea' stops tugging at my attention as it has been captured in ten or twenty minutes of creation for the future. And this opens up the space for meeting the deadline as I'm not distracted by other ideas.

When it comes to the future time, most of the work is done for bringing an idea to fruition, in ways that are far faster and easier than if I leave it until later and am trying to remember the good idea I had so long ago. If you create while the energy is there it will speed up your capacity for creating and you'll have more ease. You just need a great system for retrieving your work. I have a personal love affair with Scrivener. It's writer's software and it was built for the way my brain files and rearranges information. I use it for a lot more than just writing.

STOP WAITING, START CREATING

A lot of people ask me about how to have flow with deadlines, as if the deadline is all that matters. What's interesting about deadlines is that they are rarely inflexible and rarely a matter of life and death. I choose to work with people who are flexible, who are willing to embrace flow, who know that they'll get a better result if they create when the energy is there. Sometimes you have to talk to your clients or your boss about how you work. Your approach to having flow with deadlines needs to work for everyone, or it will work for no-one ultimately.

I no longer operate from the idea that 'whoever screams loudest or longest' gets my attention. That is a sure way to turn your life into a constant stream of needy people whose needs you have placed above your creative energies. Urgent is not a priority, it's a choice that you don't have to make if you're willing to be aware!

Some people create from force because they think that is the only way to create. That there can't be any pleasure in creating. I did a live-stream event and I'm still bemused by the beautiful person that said "What? Creating can be pleasurable? I'd rather clean the toilet floor with a toothbrush!" She was one of many people that believe that if you are in flow and it is fun then something MUST. BE. WRONG. No, that is the myth of the suffering artist. It's just a choice whether you indulge in the pleasure of creating, or the pain of forcing creation!

Flow is a space of synchronicity, serendipity and ease. Flow is where we change one molecule and the entire Universe moulds to our desires. Flow is play. Flow is not 'go with the flow and never create anything'. That's not flow, that's floating blind. Be aware, there are rapids approaching! 'Going with the flow' is where you don't make choices or create anything you desire; it is where you

Lisa Murray

allow whatever comes to come and then complain that you don't have what you desire. It is totally different to enjoying the active flow of making choices, being present with what is required of you and allowing your desires to come to you with ease.

In the last few seconds you have moved about 60,000 kilometres, even if it feels like you are sitting or standing still. Through the movement of the sun and the planets every molecule is constantly in motion. We can't be stuck if we connect with the molecules. There are new possibilities available in every second if we are willing to know they exist!

Are you waiting for the flow to show up? If you are sitting in a pond and the water is stagnant, then you have to look at it and go 'well, I'm in a dam, not a stream, a dam goes nowhere, it has walls, where else can I go instead?' And then you need to open the floodgates, change direction, make a leap and find your flow.

If you find you are always waiting for the future to show up, as if what you are asking for is taking too long to arrive, there is one more thing to do. Create more. A lot more!! I was always a frustrated 'waiter' as if my life could not come to fruition soon enough. I simply wasn't creating enough. When I started to ask for a lot more to show up, I took myself out of waiting mode, and into choice. When a lot of cool things show up at once, you don't have to say yes to it all. You can begin to have choice. What would be the most fun for you? What would create what you would most like to create in the world? It rarely shows up how you think it will.

Creativity

Creativity is about standing out. Being the Eva Peron, Andy Warhol, Richard Branson, Frida Kahlo, Christopher Columbus, Steve Jobs, Lady Gaga, Charles Dickens or Winston Churchill in your field - in ways that only you can. Creativity is about being a leader, whether you have followers or not.

If you're not willing to lead, you can't be creative, you can only be a copycat. Are you going to play out your beautiful, brilliant life singing old songs over and over in your own personal Elvis cover band? Or are you going to use it to shine your unique capacities far into the world, in ways that inspire others to be more of who they truly are?

I loved Graham Moore's 2015 Oscar acceptance speech: "Stay weird. Stay different. When you are standing on this stage, please pass this message along." If each of us did this, on whatever stage we are on, the world would become a much more joyful place to live. Difference isn't wrong. Don't get bent out of shape because you are different. Embrace it. Make it your gift instead of your limitation.

Creativity shows up when you see the world different to other people. You join seemingly unrelated dots in unfathomable and unexpected ways. You create something new, beyond what already exists. Creativity is not about unashamedly copying other people's ideas (badly) or making things pretty (although that can be part of it if you choose!).

Lisa Murray

Creativity is living YOUR life as only you can. It's being the difference you truly be, rather than trying to be like everyone else. It's creating a business that delights you, or finding work you love where your talents and abilities can be a contribution that is appreciated. It's bringing the new into being. It's bringing YOU into being.

We hide our creativity so people won't judge us. The good news is, they'll judge us no matter what we choose. What if our care factor about other people's judgements could be totally non-existent? Changing this one thing will unlock so much creative energy you'll be making the Energiser Bunny look like he's taking a long nap! You know what to do with judgement (Remember we talked about turning it into gratitude!)... do it! And set yourself free!

Tenacity {Surprise! There's a Sixth Element!}

A tenacity to keep going underpins all of the other elements. Not to keep going in that way that long-suffering artists do. Not in the way of flogging your worn out rocking horse to death. But to keep creating. To keep discovering fresh perspectives. To know that you will get where you're going, whatever it takes. To never give up on yourself, even when you can only see the barest tip of the iceberg forming.

Tenacity is the oil that allows us to slide and glide forward through even the tiniest cracks and crevices, rather than tumbling down hills and over rocks, only to begin the climb once more. You only start from the beginning (again) if you aren't willing to receive the contribution of every choice you've ever made.

I am always in a process of reinvention and expansion. Nothing is static or stuck because I don't allow it to be so. Tenacity is the energy of always moving forward, even if there is no path. Even if you're blinded by snowstorms, hurricanes and tornadoes. Tenacity is knowing where you are going, and choosing to go there, even if 'there' is so undefinable you feel like you are crazy.

This is an energy I am intimately familiar with. I cannot tell you how many times I've wondered what the hell I'm creating all of this for, only to have someone send me a message of how I made a difference to them in exactly the right moment. Tenacity is about committing to your life. Never letting anyone or anything stop you. It is the choice that has allowed me to create my 'impossible future', even through the depths of despair. Tenacity is you, being the phoenix that rises from the ashes. Having the courage to start wherever you are and keep going to where you desire to go.

When you have a dream, you know it's possible. Even if every person around you thinks otherwise. You KNOW it's possible. What you might not know is that most likely it will come to fruition in a totally different way than what you imagined. If you're willing, it will show up even greater. This is not the moment to say 'I told you so' to your naysayers. It's the moment to ask 'what can I create that is even more phenomenal than this?" That is a much more fun way of delivering 'I told you so' ;) AND it offers them the possibility to choose what they would love to create too. What if your tenacity in having what you desire can be an invitation to people around you to choose something different?

There's an energy you can add to tenacity that changes it from struggle to flow. The energy of ease! Mostly there are at least 20,000 ways to create any idea we have, but we have only learned one or two ways, so we limit how we create and what is possible. The naysayers are not willing to look outside the box of force, control and necessity. The creators ask "If I was going to create this with ease, how would it be different?"

I created the foundation of this book by running Creativity Lab events all over Europe. It was so much fun! When I started to write, the words flowed with ease because I had already talked about many of the concepts. Listening to the replays of the events showed me exactly what people need to know. I didn't have to work it out!

STOP WAITING, START CREATING

And when I gave people sample chapters to read, the feedback has been "I felt like you were talking directly to me." This is the ease of creating!

Ease is not created from the assumption of 'There is all this stuff to be done, I don't have a choice, I just have to plough my way through it.' Instead you can ask 'What's next?' What's going to create the most ease here?' And then follow the energy, rather than the logic. The tenacity comes from continuing to ask the question. From committing to the creation of your idea.

And please know, it is totally okay to go 'okay I'm done with this idea, I'm going to create something else instead.' That is not failure. That is awareness of what is going to work for your future. And know that some ideas come and go. I've been in and out of love with my business coaching business at different times and it is always showing me how it would love to be more and contribute more in my life. Everything has its season, you don't have to be full steam ahead on everything all of the time. Some things grow greater when you allow them to lie fallow for a while. That's not giving up - it's being aware of a different possibility.

Ignore the naysayers and the judgement police. They are not living your life! Someone said to me 'If you could do anything with your life, what would you choose?' And, I replied "write fiction books and let them support me in the way I'd like to become accustomed to." I wasn't joking. To me this is a future reality that I am already starting to create.

They said "You can't do that!" And I responded, "Just watch me!!" Now, I have no idea how that will show up or work, but I know that if that is what I'm choosing, that is what will be created. The creative process often starts when we least expect it. I was on a flight to Europe from Australia, almost everyone was asleep, and the idea for a movie script arrived in my awareness. I very quickly realised it's part of my fiction empire. I sat up, turned on the light and in around 20 minutes wrote out every detail I could remember. The writing will come when it comes, the idea has been formed.

If you have an idea that is always on your heels, that you are always loving, that makes you come alive… stick with it. No matter how crazy people think you are. It's your life, not theirs.

****** EXPLORATION ******

Let's add each of these elements to one of your projects that is not moving forward as you desire, to see what can show up in a different way. Choose a project or an idea that needs love… and add each of the creation elements we've explored in this chapter by asking the questions that you usually refuse to ask because they don't fit your pre-determined assumptions about what you are creating.

1. Spontaneity, not planning.

If I wasn't planning this and I was willing to destroy all current plans, what could I choose right now that would move this forward? What would be the most fun for me with this project today?

STOP WAITING, START CREATING

2. Flexibility, not resistance to change.
What am I refusing to change, that if I change it, would open up more possibilities than I am currently aware of? What have I decided is correct and real that is not? What one thing can I alter right now that would allow this to move forward faster?

3. Exploration and experimentation, not being a 'know-it-all'.
What do I think I know about this that is not true? What could I know about this that I haven't been willing to know? What could I question here that I have not ever questioned before? What is supposed to be impossible that I could create just for fun?

4. Flow, not force.
What am I trying to force that is not working? What can I be or do different that would allow the flow to show up with total ease? What flow can I invite that I've been refusing, so I can keep suffering and struggling?

5. Creativity, not copying.
What difference am I or can I add to this that would make it totally different to what exists in the world right now? What is the difference I've been unwilling to choose that could totally change this?

Lisa Murray

6. Tenacity!
Have a Finishathon. Bring your idea into the world as only you can!

Through Access Consciousness® I learned that asking the questions that no-one else has the courage to ask creates new choices and possibilities which create the forward movement you are asking for. These questions may or may not have obvious answers. When you ask them, you open the doors that offer even more choices and possibilities. Questions create!!

~SECTION 2~
WHAT ARE YOU CREATING?

CREATIVE CLARITY: CHOOSING WHAT TO CREATE

"What choices do you have that other people don't have?" ~ **Gary Douglas**

Does creating give you energy and expand your Universe, or do you prefer to just 'keep on going' even if you feel like dying most days? Is NOT creating actually sucking the life out of you?

Seven years ago I had severe burnout. I couldn't hold a conversation and I couldn't stay out of bed for more than about three hours at a time. I could not see any possibilities for creating beyond where I was in my life (which looked great on the surface!). Except it was killing me - literally!

What changed everything for me and gave me a new life far beyond what I ever imagined, was beginning to create from a totally different space.

Lisa Murray

Before the burnout I would create because I could. I would contribute because I knew how. I would create because I was aware of a different possibility. And most of all I created from necessity. I was so acutely aware of the projections and expectations of others, that all I ever did was fulfil the needs of the people around me. Exhaustion was just the start of what I was actually creating. Not my brightest choice. (Lucky I'm cute!!)

What changed the burnout and the 'less than' choices I was making was the choice to create for me. The choice to create beyond what I knew. The choice to create from possibilities rather than problems.

My new sense of creating started small. I began to write every day. That simple daily practice has leapt and grown into so much more than I ever imagined. My writing reaches thousands of people now. And writing led to speaking... and speaking is leading to all sorts of amazing possibilities for creating that I never imagined possible not so long ago. So a seemingly 'small' choice was actually a big one! How does it get even better?

And the choices that seemed the biggest on the surface have often created the least for me. Now, my perspective on big choices and small choices is entirely different! I've stopped creating the 'less than' choices that fit me neatly into other people's realities. I'm not looking for the choices that other people consider big, I'm asking for the choices that will create the most change and possibilities in MY world. It's different. Really different!

I have a question for you. When you allow your life to be 'less than' is that a contribution to a creative, generative, sustainable future, or is it a way of pretending that you are small, weak and powerless and can't change anything that truly matters?

STOP WAITING, START CREATING

If you are anything like me, you've been known to tell yourself all sorts of crazy stories about what you can't be, do or create and yet, when you ask that brilliant Access Consciousness® question: "If I create this what will the world be like in 50 years, 100 years or 500 years?" it becomes difficult to ignore the contribution you truly could be and receive!!

In acknowledging all I already know about creating, I am also aware that I haven't truly even scratched the surface yet... there is so much more to discover! Creating is the adventure of living for me. It's the possibility of expanding far beyond anything that has ever existed. It's what allows me to thrive in the moment, rather than pretend I'm dying.

What is creating for you? Would you be willing to perceive and receive a different possibility for your reality and the world?

The 'What To Create?' Question

We all go through stages where 'what to create?' is the burning question. There are either so many ideas you can't decide where to start (or what to finish!) or a you are in a vacuum of 'no ideas' that is sucking so hard you can feel your insides doing somersaults out of frustration! The cool thing about both of these situations is that they are often just showing you where there is a lack of information.

Whenever I'm frustrated or overwhelmed I ask 'What else can I be aware of that would change this?' It's amazing what shows up and how quickly those energies can shift! So this chapter is all about the questions you can ask to receive more information that will lead you to where you'd like to go!

If you could choose to create anything, what would it be? A lot of people say 'more time' or 'balance' or 'freedom'. What if you are actually asking for more space? Or to have the space for creating? Creating is a pleasurable activity. We get to be who we truly are and it makes us happy. And yet, most people resist it as if it's a contagious disease. Are you creating your life as too busy to allow yourself to get happy? Are you always in search of 'balance' as if that will offer the perfect answer to your cravings?

Balance isn't something I aspire to. Balance is a trade-off between two (or more) things. That sucks! What if you could have all of it? My target is to have space, not balance. The space to create, the space to explore, the space to enjoy living, the space to BE, the space to choose a new adventure in any moment. Space is the new bliss.

Start With Your Brilliance, Not Your Passion

Your brilliance is what you have the capacity to create, beyond what exists. It's where you create what no-one else can. Your passion is described as being about what you love. Most of us love things that are hard, full of struggle and stress. And if you are thinking 'oh no, that's not me', take a look at your life. If it is that way, that is what you love creating.

STOP WAITING, START CREATING

So many people would like to escape their job, to live their life doing something they love. It's totally possible. But if you start with your passion, you could get stuck there, and it might not be nearly as much fun as you imagine. And if you are hating on me for saying that right now, stay with me into the next chapter, you'll be so glad you did! 'Follow your passion' is one of the myths that do us over in our search for the perfect life. Let's explore your brilliance first!

When I was 15 I decided I'd like to be a chef. I loved to cook and so I did work experience at a local restaurant. It was one of my best ever choices. I very quickly realised I was not going to enjoy cooking for 60 hours a week in a busy kitchen. For me cooking is about pleasure, about putting flavours and textures together with a glass of wine in hand, licking the bowl, watching people's faces as they enjoy the food, experimenting on my friends and creating new recipes. This melting-moment kind of cooking bears almost no resemblance to the fast-paced energy of a commercial kitchen. I had a lucky escape. I still love cooking. And I'm so happy to say 'no thank you' every time someone suggests I open a cafe. There are some things you want to keep as pleasures to love - because you can.

If you are obsessed with the idea of making your hobbies into your paid work - do your hobby day in day out for a week or three. And begin to create it as a business - with all of the 'extra' elements that a business requires (like finding customers). Ask yourself, do you still want to do it as your work? Or is the joy already starting to diminish?

You don't need to get paid for everything you love. A lot of people try to make money from projects and ideas that would be better as hobbies. They love their cool amazing thing, but it's not their true zone of brilliance and what they are offering is not different enough from what already exists for people to trust them with their money. So the money doesn't flow as easily as it could. To be financially successful you either need to get brilliant at doing or creating what you love, or get awesome at marketing your brilliance (or both!). There is always a way to create what you truly desire.

You need to be willing to be paid for your brilliance, unless you're going to keep it as a hobby. For years I did business coaching for friends over a glass of wine. I didn't know it was called business coaching. I just knew that when they asked me questions about their business it was really easy for me to give them the information that would change the situation. It was fun for me. It was only when I got burnout that I discovered that I could get paid for this. Man, was I excited!!! To think I'd been working my ass off for other people for all this time... when I could have been having inspiring conversations with people creating interesting things in the world and getting paid for it!

It was like Christmas a thousand times over... until I realised that most coaches aren't crazy enough to see six clients a day. My coaching sessions tend to shift a lot of energy - they were long and intense days, often with lots of driving. There was one particular day when I was driving home and I went very close to falling asleep at the wheel. I was beyond tired. And yet, once I'd been home about an hour, my energy returned to its usual high levels. I found this a little strange so I asked a few questions of my body. Turns out I loved the coaching, but my body was not quite as excited. So I reinvented my approach to one-on-one coaching almost immediately. I do a lot less of it now - and that could change at any time!

Listening to these subtle signs is what true creating is about. Choosing something until you don't. It's not about finding 'the answer' or the 'one thing' that is going to keep you happy for the rest of your life. About 15 years ago I read a book by Marcus Letcher called *Making Your Future Work* where he talked about having multiple interests and jobs. At the time that was a very innovative idea, in just a few years it's almost become 'normal'. Contrary to popular opinion, creating isn't about choosing the one 'right' answer. It's about inviting an ever-changing array of ideas and projects into life. The other great thing that occurs if you choose to be what I describe as 'multi-creative' is that money comes from many different projects. When you aren't relying on an employer or a couple of big clients for your cash-flow you are creating true financial freedom.

A lot of people make themselves wrong for having many projects. Or you might shift and change your ideas every few days or weeks or months. It truly doesn't matter anywhere near as much as people say. They only want you to define you so that they can confine you into the box of their judgement. Is that what is going to work for you?

I've had people try to make me wrong for changing how I connect with clients. Their judgement was 'you should do what works for me!' Even when I explained that the strategy they were suggesting was not working for my life at the time, they persisted. My point of view was 'watch me out-create your limitations'. What if you would give the naysayers the armchair adventure of watching you living beyond their 'rules' instead?

I have been judged my whole life for changing my mind. Apparently I do it far too often for most people's comfort. The funny thing is, this is one of my greatest creative capacities. My willingness to change direction in any moment allows for my creative energies to show up with a lot more ease. The more you choose this, the greater you will become at creating from 'nothing'. Of course, you never start with nothing (you ALWAYS have you!) even so, it can feel like it sometimes.

Let's Get Specific. What Are You Going To Create?

What would YOU love to create? Maybe something totally new and unexpected flashed through your awareness. More likely you came up with the tired old list of expectations of yourself that you've been carrying around for years. What if you would just put that list aside and ask yourself what it would be like to be on the creative edge of possibilities instead? The creative edge is all about choice. It's the thrill of the leap, rather than the stupefying faux satisfaction of following the herd.

Creating is about being curious. Making different choices. Write down the ideas that come, even if they seem ludicrous or crazy. Ideas become more tangible in random, spontaneous and surprising ways. You don't 'work ideas out', you adore them into being. What if creating is a nurturing adventure rather than a limiting book of rules? Don't let your creative flames be suffocated by rules. Fan the fire and fuel it up!

STOP WAITING, START CREATING

We tend to categorise the things we would like to create into the possible or the impossible... As a child I read every fantasy book I could get my hands on. I knew there was more to the world than what I could see. It's easy to judge what is beyond our imagination as impossible or unreal. But is it? Imagine what could be possible if you would allow yourself to venture into the far reaches of fantasy, into the dimensions of dragons, unicorns, fairies and all kinds of other so-called 'mythological' inspirations.

I know, you don't want to leave planet earth. But what if Goethe was right? What if earth IS the mental institution for the entire Universe? What if there are multiverses of possibilities and we have been limiting ourselves to only what we can see?

What then? I am fairly sure that Einstein did not limit his thinking to what he could see, just as our bodies don't limit what they receive to what they can see. (You know... that sweet thing called the air we breathe... we can't see that either, and yet, it exists!)

Okay... maybe you aren't quite ready for creating like a genius would just yet! So let's start with what we like to call reality... it is a reality... if not the only one! What can you create in the reality you are most familiar with?

Lisa Murray

A Creative Project?

"I'd asked around 10 or 15 people for suggestions. Finally one lady friend asked the right question, 'Well, what do you love most?' That's how I started painting money." ~ **Andy Warhol**

There are a lot of frustrated creatives in the world. We are born creative and then we go to school. In most cases we are judged for our creations and so we learn not to create. Then we go to work and are judged some more. Is it any wonder we don't embrace our creative energies? Artists are often seen as starving hippies who should get a job. The creation of beauty is not valued unless you can put a multi-million dollar business around it (the fashion industry being a great example of this).

The weird thing is, we are always creating. We can choose to do it with elegance, beauty and creativity or we can create from the energy of fast and boring will do as long as the job gets done. I'd like to invite you to a different possibility. One where you create for the pleasure of creating. It might be an artwork, a book, a garden, a meal, or computer software that will change the world. What 'it' is isn't nearly as important as the way you create and your willingness to share it with the world. Sometimes I write in a frenzy, totally obsessed with word

STOP WAITING, START CREATING

count. Other days I write more slowly, savouring each word and making sure it matches the exact energy I would like to represent.

Getting creative allows you to express who you truly are. You don't have to be good at it (it's not everyone's zone of brilliance), you just have to be willing to enjoy the creative process. This is one way into discovering your personal creative flow. And once you can tap into flow with ease, you can create almost anything at will. Get some materials and make a mess... create something that you can throw away if it's not what you imagined it could be. What if destruction isn't wrong? Discover what else a creative project can offer. It's a way of becoming more present in the world. Your presence makes a difference, especially when you are having a good time creating!

I have a 'Writing Wild' program that is used by a lot of creatives that don't write as their main form of creativity. Being willing to embrace one form of creativity leads to creativity in many other areas. Choose to paint, draw, sing, model, yodel, sculpt, write or construct... your choice of materials is less relevant than that you awaken the energies of creation.

And of course there is also energetic creation - where you create with the intangible but real energies that can contribute to your creations. This will be covered in my next book - *Conscious Creating*. You can also enjoy a preview with my free "Creative Alchemy" e-class. Find it at www.CreativityLab.tv/Alchemy

Lisa Murray

Are You Creating A Business?

"Being good in business is the most fascinating kind of art. Making money is art and working is art and good business is the best art." - **Andy Warhol**

Most people avoid creating a business because they put all of the emphasis on the business. And business has been created as something that is not playful and not fun. What the...? What were those business people thinking? That something is more valuable if it is serious? Not in my world. I value play! And I include my businesses as part of my creative energies.

A business is just another form of creation. I don't do business by the commonly espoused rules, and nor should you. That is not creative, that is what causes misery and boredom! If you question every element of how business is done, you'll begin to create your business from a totally different space! The space of you being authentically you in the world.

Your business can show you what to create if you are willing to listen. Since I started business coaching, I have asked for the clients to find me who can show me what is next for my business. This one question has delivered me the most amazing clients, and the most fun and ease-filled way of creating my businesses.

STOP WAITING, START CREATING

Here's the thing that is most important if you would like to create from this space. You've got to get really, really good at listening. Listening is more than just using your ears. It's a form of following the energy of what's possible, and choosing from there.

I'm not talking about Listening 101 where you pretend you heard someone by parroting back their words. I'm talking about true listening. Being aware of the spoken and the unspoken. Asking questions about people's dreams and desires. Perceiving future possibilities. And knowing when something sounds like a good idea on the surface, but is not likely to come to fruition. In my Business Alchemy and Nurture Project programs we play with listening in entirely new ways!

Most people see almost nothing of what is available. An architect told me she spent six months of her training learning to look up. Most people see paintings in 2D, like a postcard, when in reality they are filled with all kinds of information and energies. What if you could perceive everything, and simply hone in on what is relevant to what you would like to create and what the world is asking for? It's possible - it takes a request to perceive everything, and a willingness to do so.

Most people do not clearly articulate what they are truly asking for. If you 'listen' with awareness, you'll get a sense of the underlying energies, and you'll be able to create adventures and ideas and projects that will thrill the people you play with. If your community love your ideas, you will love creating for them. This is a platform of infinite creation that builds on itself if you will allow it to grow.

One way to start is to look at the questions people ask you. Then go into the wonderful wondering space of

Lisa Murray

'what would be fun to create?' and allow the ideas to pop. Mostly there is something sitting right in front of your face. Often I will run a trial version of my idea first with just a few of the core elements - to see if it is interesting to people and to make sure it is going to be as fun as I imagine! Over the years I have run so many different experiments - sometimes for curiosity, sometimes to receive more information, always to invite people to a more playful way of creating.

I also look at what I desire to change and create in the world. Often my audience is not ready for that immediately, but I love to add elements of these possibilities into what I create. It offers them new possibilities and it begins the energy of creation.

How do you start a business? By helping one person get where they would like to go and having them pay you for it. While most of us would love to start with a grand plan and multi-million dollars in venture capital, you have to start wherever you can. I know some brilliant people, with brilliant ideas, that have wasted years and years of their life because they don't have the funding to create the idea they have made more valuable than anything. There is always another way… or another idea! Go find it. Stop waiting!!!

And please be clear - you don't have a business until people are buying what you are offering. Are you getting paid for your hobby? Or are you running a business? Neither one is right or wrong, and it's always a good idea to know which one it is. (The tax office prefers that kind of clarity too.)

Think of five to ten people who who you would LOVE to have as clients. What can you create that will take them where they truly desire to go? Start there.

And if you desire to create your business unconventionally, check out Business Alchemy Lab - www.BusinessAlchemyLab.com. It's an adventure in creating your business intuitively.

Are You Creating Your Life?

"As soon as you trust yourself, you will know how to live." ~ **Johann Wolfgang von Goethe**

I went through a fairly miserable phase a few years ago when nothing was working, no matter what I did, no matter how hard I worked. I had totally lost trust in myself and I was angry and confused. In a particularly impressive melt-down moment (maybe you'd call it a tantrum), a mentor gave me some tough love - 'go and create your life' he said, and not nearly as politely as that! At the time I was perplexed. I thought that was what I was doing. No. I was creating crap by listening to people who did not know what was best for me, even though they meant well and thought they did. There's quite a difference between creating a life YOU would love to live, and creating the life other people think you should live.

I came to discover that creating my life meant waking up in the morning and making choices that would work for me. My first choice was to ask a question that I learned through Access Consciousness: 'What's it going to take to out-create myself today?' I asked that question every day for over 18 months and my life changed dramatically in that time. It was a rare day that something amazing didn't show up. Which was in stark contrast to the 18 months before that. Every choice we make creates the possibility for change.

With the 'go create your life' mantra in mind, I would ask the question and then follow the energy of whatever felt light. A new friend asked would I travel from Australia to Stockholm to offer a Creativity Lab event. On a week's notice I said yes, even though the logistics were insane. That one choice created many amazing possibilities into the future. The following year I took this work into ten countries and discovered so much about creating that I never would have known if I hadn't gone travelling. When you out-create yourself, nothing stays the same! I never have the point of view that I have my life or my business 'right'. There is always something more I can create.

Creating your life includes all kinds of things... it could be diving deep into living your bucket list of travels and adventures, creating relationships or friendships, creating space to connect with the planet, creating the awareness to be truly YOU, creating a home you adore, or even creating a life where you have total choice and freedom. Whatever it is for you there is one thing I know. The only way you'll create your dreams is if you start!

Creating your life won't show up how you think it will. Start asking questions and see what you would like to choose. If you would like some questions to play with, see www.CreativityLab.tv/QuestionsCreate for more!

What you create is a choice. You can't get it wrong. You can only have adventures. Let's start creating!

How Do You Start?.... YOU. JUST. START!

'Too' Much Creative Energy and No Idea Where To Put It?

Have you ever woken up with lots of creative energy, a burning desire to create something - anything - and yet no idea of what you'd like to create? And then you get disheartened watching all of that creative energy just kind of burn itself into nothing, rather than becoming a contribution to you and your life. What happened? You didn't make a choice. So your creative energy fizzled out.

What do you do when you're full of beans and there's no obvious play-space to start from? You ask that yummy bouncy energy to show you what's possible. You don't limit your creating to what you already know you can't create (which is what most of us do!)

So what is it you know about what you'd like to create that you've been pretending you don't know?

I went from having no ideas to having about a trillion more ideas than I could ever hope to create in this lifetime. What changed? My willingness to start! Anywhere! The first few (hundred) ideas were false starts. I found myself creating things that were great in theory but weren't quite enough fun for me once I started.

So I quit them - no regrets, no backward glances, no wrongness of me. Every time I discovered something new about how and what I'd like to create. Each 'false start' was a gift in disguise. Despite the assertions of many a so-called guru, there is no recipe for knowing what to create, just questions, a vivid imagination, some sense of future possibilities and a willingness to join dots that others don't even see!

As Gary Douglas says "choice creates awareness, awareness doesn't create choice." We think we have to have the awareness first. No, that's a form of waiting. If you start with a choice, that will open more doors than you knew existed.

Your First Priority Is To START!

"Whatever you can do or dream you can, begin it. Boldness has genius, power and magic in it!" ~ **Johann Wolfgang von Goethe**

To begin creating, you can ask the question "What's next?" And literally do the next thing that pops into your awareness. When you have enough of that, ask again: "What's next?" and continue like that for an entire day (or week or year or lifetime… it's your choice).

You might start by looking out the window and watching the birds. How can they inspire you? Then you might go for a walk. How can that inspire you? Then you might hang out in a cafe, eavesdropping. How can that inspire you? If you become aware of the world with fresh senses, the possibilities for creation expand dynamically.

STOP WAITING, START CREATING

The space where you are least likely to be creative is at your desk. I prefer not to create at my desk. Mostly I move around the house and often I go out. My 'Merry Christmas to me' gift one year was a full-length outdoor beanbag. Some days I move it around the backyard, following the sun or the shade. By asking my body to contribute to what I'm creating, I get an awareness of where the most creative energies will be for me. Some days it's the beach, other days a quiet creek near where I live. Sometimes I need to have cafe buzz filling up my five senses so that my uncommon senses can switch on. I am happy almost anywhere, as long as I'm creating!

Different cities offer different energies too. I went to Berlin on a whisper of the future. I knew there was something there for me. I felt creative from the moment I landed. I went to a conference full of creative people and everything pointed to one thing: WRITE! So I have been! On my third visit to Berlin I went to the David Bowie exhibition that was based in part on his creative sabbatical there. It got me inspired in so many different ways! When you find a space that supports your creative energies, do whatever you can to invite that into your life! How? By making a choice to go with what you know. San Francisco invites me into that energy of creation. My trips there aren't at all logical and yet, it has been a contribution to many of my creative projects!

Creating begins with the art of the start. It finishes whenever we choose. When we are being a perfectionist it is our judgement that decides when something is complete. When we are creating from a space of wonder and curiosity, it is our awareness that lets us know when our project is finished. Most people spend so much time wondering where to start that they never actually start.

Lisa Murray

While I am saying 'start anywhere', there is also the risk of starting everywhere and getting nowhere. Random creation is the energy of 'start anywhere'. It is useful to get started, and then you need to make choices that will actively move your projects forward into fruition. It's just like this book — I had the awareness this would be the first book to be published, even though I had another one almost finished. And it was a great choice to make - even if it wasn't logical at the time. So much has fallen together with ease since then that it's been a truly magical creative experience. You have to make choices and continue to create towards those choices. Otherwise you end up with hundreds of unfinished ideas and no money — not so much fun.

Where you start depends on your priorities. For some people, having money coming in is essential (don't leave your day job just yet). For others, what is essential is to enjoy the process, or to create an idea that has momentum in the world, or to know they can create something from start to finish. For me, I tend to create by having 30-50 projects going at once, and following the energy of which ones to give the greatest attention to. I have just one rule. I can only start a new project in any given month if I finish one of the existing projects first. It keeps me in the energy of finishing just as much as starting… and you know what that means. Joy! Celebration! Bliss!

What you create is not as important as the questions you ask along the way. The questions and your 'what' need to connect. If your highest priority is to enjoy the process, but the question you are always asking is 'How can I make money?' then you may find you are going in circles, with neither request showing up. Here are a few ways to get started.

STOP WAITING, START CREATING

If your priority is to produce income ask: "What can I put my energy and attention today that will produce income for now and the future?" Find the project that has the most possibility for income - move it forward in every moment that you can until it is ready to be launched into the world. This does not mean becoming a workaholic. My best ideas come when I go hangout at the beach or with a horse, or when I'm standing aimlessly in the shower, staring at the wall.

You can also go grab my free 'Creating Money' mini e-course available at www.CreativityLab.tv/CreatingMoney - it has some very different strategies for inviting money into your life! What if working ever harder is not the answer to creating money?

If your priority is to enjoy the process of creating, ask 'What can I create today that would give me more ease and joy than ever before?' You might be surprised at what shows up... what if you like creating order? Or creating happiness for your body? Or creating gardens? Or a website? Or creating ideas that have not yet existed? And maybe all of this could be rolled together?? Enjoying the process is about being 1000% present with what you are creating. Being totally in the now and including your body, your being and (if you must!) your brain! A great way to get into the process of creating is to explore my 'Writing Wild' free e-course (available at www.creativitylab.tv/writingwild). I've had people say it unlocked and unleashed their creativity far beyond words.

If your priority is to create a global movement for change, ask 'What is the world asking of me that I've not yet been willing to create?' or 'What conversations would I love to have in the world that no-one else is having?" The awareness that shows up may surprise you and your capacities for creating may expand very quickly. A movement is not created with just one person. You also need to ask 'Where are the people that would like to co-create this with me? What can I create that will invite them to play?"

"The power to question is the basis of all human progress." ~ **Indira Gandhi**

In almost all kinds of education you are taught to ask questions that you can easily get the answer to. And you are judged intensively for not knowing 'the answer'. Allowing yourself to be creative and innovative comes from behaving in the opposite way to what you have been taught. Allowing yourself to 'not know' before you ask. Every single thing you would like to create can be created by asking questions that you don't have the answer to. Asking a question opens doorways to the infinite. Defining an answer is how you close doors. Answers create a set of finite limitations.

Refuse To Do It 'Right'

Creating is not about getting it 'right'. There is no rightness or wrongness to creation... I still create things before the world is ready for them. And if I don't make myself wrong for that, something greater is always created. It's only when I'm desperately trying to 'get it

STOP WAITING, START CREATING

right' that the energy of creation doesn't show up for me. What would you create if you couldn't get it wrong?

What could you create if you were to deliberately create something badly? If ever I'm having a moment of not being able to write, I start by writing badly. Writing rubbish. Writing the kind of trash that makes 50 Shades of Grey look like a literary masterpiece. (Maybe I should get a pen name.) That kind of 'bad' opens up the possibilities for all kinds of 'good'.

We have been blamed, shamed and guilted into feeling embarrassed to even try. I've discovered something really amazing. If I don't make myself wrong, then what other people think becomes totally irrelevant. It is only when I judge my creations that their judgements start to matter to me in any way.

Love your creations, no matter how 'right' or 'wrong' they are. I am not the world's best painter. But I love to paint... walls, furniture, pictures, colours... it really doesn't matter to me. Adding paint to any kind of surface makes me happy. When I had burnout, I spent the first few weeks at home (very slowly) painting walls. It was a way of allowing my brain to unwind from the intensity of stress and overwhelm I had put it through. Painting is one of the ways I stop thinking. I probably would have died of a brain implosion without it. I didn't care about getting the painting 'right'. I was using it to keep myself alive. No-one (even me) really knew that at the time.

There is no space for judgement in creation. If you are grateful for the outcomes, even if they are nothing like you imagined, another possibility is always created.

Lisa Murray

Start Being Creative In Every Detail Of Your Life

In some ways, this way of starting the creation process is often the one we resist least. Maybe because it's simple. More likely because we think these 'little' things don't matter. They aren't 'big' choices, but they make life infinitely more beautiful.

If you are giving someone a gift, wrap it in a quirky way. If you are writing a report at work, inject a little humour in appropriate places. If you are talking to a friend, don't censor yourself to fit in with their judgements.

If you create from home, make your space visually delicious and physically comfortable. Stop 'making do' with bits of leftover furniture. I was momentarily inspired to make everything more beautiful when I got an Instagram account. Taking photos was a way of seeing my environment from new perspectives. It opened my eyes to the beauty that is everywhere. And it started to inform my creative work in new ways too. Sometimes the simplest things inspire us to create.

When you use every moment of your life as a creative possibility you immerse yourself in the joy and ease of creating. It is no longer 'a big thing' to create. Creating becomes as easy as breathing - and you can do it as often if you choose!

Are you still stuck on having too many ideas to create? We'll talk more about that when we get into Exploring Your Creative Process in Section Three.

****** EXPLORATION ******

You have just landed on planet earth. You don't know how it works here. You have no preconceived ideas. Everything is new. Everything is an adventure. You know you are cared for and that no matter what you choose, your life will work out better than you can imagine. Now begin to ask some questions:

What would you truly love your life to be like?

If you could be you, without reference to anyone else, without any limits (like time or money or your head-trips), what would you create?

Where would you start?

PURPOSE, PASSION, PROFIT... OR PLAY?

Purpose. Passion. Profit. We hear these words bandied around everywhere, like if you get the right answer to those three things, your life will be perfect. No. It won't. You will just be happy because you think you've finally got it right! Until the moment you realise it was right for a minute, but it's not anymore! The sad thing is, we rarely hear the word play. It seems to be reserved for children. I wonder what children can teach us about creating and being creative?

When Rumi wrote *"Let yourself be silently drawn by the strange pull of what you really love. It will not lead you astray."* He did not say "Do what you love and the money will come" or "Get paid for your passion." In the last few years we have heard this said over and over by every internet marketer trying to sell their over-priced products under the guise of freedom.

Rumi was inviting you to a life where you *"respond to every call that excites your spirit."* This kind of invitation leads to a deep wealth of creation that goes far beyond money. And it is a way of following the energy of play towards that which will make you deeply happy, rather than surface-level happy.

Your Passion

'Following your passion' is how you get your life 'right' according to many current thought leaders. They are well intentioned and they are leading people into choices that don't often work as expected.

Almost every week someone looks at the magic of my life and asks me 'how do I follow my passion?'. My first response is to ask 'what is passion to you?' All sorts of answers are given, but it's rare to find anyone who knows the meanings of the word 'passion'. If you're wondering why 'finding your passion' has felt so excruciating, here it is, straight from the dictionary:

◆ Strong and barely controllable emotion.
◆ Lust or strong sexual desire.
◆ The suffering and death of Jesus.

Well, that's a bundle of bliss right there! Or maybe not!!

The earliest use of the word passion referred to the crucifixion. It is this energy that the word passion carries. You could call it semantics, but all words have an underlying energy. When we use words to create, we are creating from those underlying energies. We always receive the energy of what we ask for - we just aren't always cognitively aware of exactly what we have asked for! I use old dictionaries a lot. It saves me from creating stupid things that aren't exactly what I really desire to create.

I see a lot of people getting very emotional about their passion not paying well enough to live, suffering in their work or being crucified by the choices they have made. (Not that I've ever done any of that ;)) Would you be willing to give up seeking your passion? What if creating anew in each moment could be a far more generative approach? What if playing with possibilities would take you where you would love to go? Even if you don't know where that is yet?

I love seeing people set themselves free after they realise what they have been asking for has not been what they truly desired. 'Ask and you shall receive' is a truth. If you ask for your passion you really are asking for it... and not in a way that will bring you joy!

Don't panic... there are other ways to create that are going to take you exactly where you are truly asking to go!

Your Purpose

As the desire to create emerges more fully, most of us play out some version of the age-old questions: "Who am I? What is my purpose?" This is another of those never-ending searches that can be a lot simpler than we have made it. What if our purpose is to fully embrace the magic of living? To immerse ourselves fully in every moment of every day, rather than living in the past or the future. What if we can't get living wrong?

One of the big things that used to stop me creating was the question about my life direction. Where were all my choices taking me? I had tried just about everything. Doing jobs I loved. Doing jobs for the money. Doing jobs for the challenge. Very expensive career counselling (that told me nothing useful). Taking jobs where I could be mentored by people who were experts in career change. Choosing random jobs just to see if I would enjoy that type of work. And after about ten years of this (it was a long pre-mid-life crisis!) I was mostly none the wiser in terms of making a specific choice that I would enjoy for longer than five minutes!

In the quest to do something more satisfying with my life, I switched my attention to psychics who specialise in life direction readings. This was far more useful. I discovered some new ideas and some talents I had been hiding for a long, long time! What was amusing about this phase was that every person I had a reading from gave me a different life purpose. A different set of ways to do what I love and make money. So now I had more choice than ever before! And for the first time, I was waking up excited about those choices and how I could invite them to play together.

Some of you will be wondering why I didn't stop after the first psychic. I had an answer, why wouldn't I stick with that? Simple. I wasn't too excited about the first answer. It seemed like a very boring way to spend the rest of my life. Do I include it in what I create? Absolutely! Is it the only idea I will ever give my creative energies to? Absolutely not! And once I realised that each person

STOP WAITING, START CREATING

would give me different information, I became curious. What else was there that I hadn't yet imagined?

No matter what we discover about our purpose, we always have choice. Ultimately our purpose is far simpler than we would like it to be. It's to live a life we love. To create the greatest possibilities from the choices we make. How we do that can change from moment to moment. We try to make it complicated, as if that will prove that we are getting it right or that we are more special than the person next to us. What if all of our self-sabotaging side-tracks are just the long way around towards the adventures of discovering something much greater?

Amongst all of this searching, I realised there was still something missing. ME! Having some directions to head in was useful, but only if I was willing to show up and be me. That has taken a little longer... It's been a lot of fun discovering who I really am! And somewhat surprising.

Let's just say that you (like me) are far greater than you imagine. Excavating that greatness and bringing it gracefully into the world is one of the true gifts of living.

If, after all of this, you are still looking for the ONE thing you would love to create (some might call it your path, your calling, your purpose) know it can be like looking for the proverbial needle in a haystack. Are you even looking in the 'right' haystack?

I thought my 'right haystack' was a job. "If only I could find the right job... then everything would be perfect." My body knew otherwise. The burnout kicked me into the most random and unexpected adventures in living I could have imagined.

Waiting for the answer to show up never works. Stumbling forward into your brilliance is way faster! And to stumble into your brilliance, you need to be willing to have spontaneous adventures, to create the unexpected happy 'accidents', to play with the extraordinary, to explore beyond anywhere you have ever been. To ask for what you have never asked for before. To create from many different spaces.

The most useful thing I've done has been to start. To try things out. To see if what I imagined something would be, could be that for me. And then to tweak like crazy. To change and shift and evolve every time I get more information on what this adventure could be.

Sometimes we get too busy trying to define our lives, rather than enjoying the adventure of nurturing and exploring the possibilities. Definition is always a limitation.

What if there are fifty or a hundred things that you would love to create? We live in an amazing Universe, we can have anything if we choose. Is having just one 'predetermined' path enough for you? If not, maybe you'd like to play more... with me and the world!

What is it you know about creating, about business, about living, that no-one else knows? You know something that no-one else on the planet is aware of. And when you start to live the life YOU would love to create, your knowing emerges out of the murky depths that you have been filling with other people's ways of living.

What conversation would you truly love to have with the world that no-one else is having? Will you start that conversation today?

STOP WAITING, START CREATING

Play... It's Not Just For Kids!

What if, instead of chasing profits, you started to chase the energy of play? Money follows joy. If you are creating your purpose or your ideas from the energy of 'I have to...' then it may be quite challenging to also be creating money through your work!

Exploring the NEW is part of playing. What is it you could try out now that you've never done before? What if it isn't about the destination but the adventure of creating. So called 'mistakes' lead to the most amazing possibilities. I can decide that I chose the 'wrong' person to promote me in a city, or I can ask to be aware of what else was created that would not otherwise have been possible. I fell in love with Amsterdam by making what initially looked like a mistake. I decided to go there anyway and it became one of the most joyful parts of that trip! I made a beautiful new friend and we were able to create many great adventures in a very short time. Making things 'wrong' creates a dead-end. Allowing yourself to play with different possibilities allows new paths to become visible.

Play is our natural state. It's the joy of living wrapped in the unique expression of who we are. I don't consider my work to be work. It is a rare day that I don't have a playful energy with it, and when play is missing, I start to ask questions about what I'm creating. Maybe it's time to create in a different way?

For those of you who still have a job, I have had jobs where there was a lot of play too. It's a matter of designing the job to work for you! It's possible when you choose to make it so. Are you willing to interview your prospective boss to see if they value having fun at work? I've been known to do that! These are the kinds of choices that create magic.

Do you remember being a child and waking up excited because every day was an adventure? You can have that energy now if you choose it. People only become old because they let go of the adventure of living.

Creativity is about play. Not logic. Not being linear. Not lining up all your ducks in a row before you start. Not about being challenged. It's about launching into the middle, having fun and exploring where you can go!

Play is about making random choices that open up unexpected doors. Choosing to move beyond the trauma of being judged as wrong, ...the security of not creating (and staying in your comfort bubble of slightly bored 'bliss'), ...the sensibleness of doing it 'the right way'. UGH! No wonder people grow old and die if this is all they are looking 'forward' to!

Go to a park or the beach and watch children playing. Are they playing 'the right way' or are they creating and playing as the energy moves them? Do they come away having had a wonderful time or do they complain that it didn't turn out how they thought it would? If you've lost the ability to play, go explore the energy of play with some kids and ask them to take you on an adventure into their world. I wonder what that could change in your world?

STOP WAITING, START CREATING

****** EXPLORATION ******

What makes you happy?

Make a list of at least 50 things that make you happy. Now, how many of those could you choose in any given day? How easy would it be to be happy in every moment? What can you choose right now that would make you happier than you've been all week?
The first time I did this I was smack-bang in the midst of burnout. I'm sad to say I could only come up with about ten things - and that was a stretch! (The first three items on the list were sleep, sleep and sleep.) I'd become so disconnected from who I truly was that I had no idea what made me happy. So that very short list was a huge incentive to start living more creatively! It was fairly clear what my no-choice Universe was creating! Not much!!

Loving Your Creations

I have a friend whose default position is procrastination. Whenever I ask about what topics around creating do you need support with, she always says 'procrastination'. She loves procrastination more than she loves creating. I love creating more than I love procrastination. That is the only difference between us. When she starts loving her creations, more creation will show up. When she starts acknowledging everything she is creating (rather than focusing on what's missing), more creation will show up. Creating is surprisingly simple if we allow it to be.

Look around you. What do you love about what you've created... in your life, in your home, in your relationships, in your friendships, in your work or business? What if you loved all of it and asked all of it to upgrade and expand? What could that create?

If there is something in your life you don't love (like your money situation, or your partner, or your boss...) it won't improve if you hate it even more! You can start to create change by having gratitude for what you have, and asking what else can change.

Remember my horse story from the "5 Elements of Creating" chapter1? I've started learning how to direct horses just using energy. When you only use energy, the horse won't move unless you have gratitude for it. Yes, you could call it horse whispering! Soon after this, I was invited to help create an amazing horse class called 'Conscious Horse, Conscious Rider' with Gary Douglas in the USA. I had already chosen to go to this class, even though I wasn't sure how it was all going to work. This invitation has made it possible - and I was invited to contribute to creating more possibilities for the Facilitators class as well... which I wasn't originally choosing to attend. When I said yes to that, my entire Universe of possibilities exploded! This is what gratitude and asking questions can create.

I don't have a 'why' for what I love! I just know how much I love hanging out with horses and what that creates in my world. Choice creates. Loving your choices creates even more. What if everything you are loving can

STOP WAITING, START CREATING

contribute to you receiving far beyond what you imagined?

Here is another example of how this works. I was asking myself a question that Gary Douglas gave me, *"What would it take to be the voice for a different reality?"* A few hours later two young boys just showed up at my door and very sweetly asked me 'Hi, would you like $3 in exchange for a $5 note?' I loved their cheeky way of asking, so I gave it to them. I asked them if the money was for them and they said yes, they wanted to get their Dad something special for Father's Day.

A few minutes later their Mum knocks on the door trying to give the money back. I told her they should keep it as I love to encourage creativity in kids. I wouldn't have given them the money if I didn't want them to have it. After a little discussion she realised she shouldn't squash their initiative and creativity either - my voice in not responding how she expected became a different reality for her. I was so happy to not make the kids wrong, not make the Mum wrong, simply to love every element of what we created together in these interactions.

We create in every single moment. I was thrilled to see how $5, a giggle-filled conversation and a different perspective can change what's possible. And it created a different future for those little boys too. Their energy was so different when they came back with their Mum. They had clearly been in trouble for their innovative approach. My response allowed them to know a different way of creating is not only okay, it's wonderful! You can't love and judge at the same time. You can't create and judge at the same time. You can love creating! You can acknowledge everything you are creating! You can have

Lisa Murray

gratitude for everything you have created, whether it worked how you expected or not!

CREATION, DESTRUCTION & CHANGE

During a three-day Creativity Lab event one of the participants said "Wow, I did not expect creating to include so much change!" She was surprised at what changed. I was surprised that it wasn't obvious that creativity and creation are underpinned by change. Maybe another example of my unconventional perspectives.

If we create from the same platforms and spaces we always have, our creative juices get a little stale. Creating is inherently about change, unless you are creating the same thing over and over and over. Is that fun for you? Or would you like to create something different every day?

If you've ever had the sense you want to die, it is worth asking whether this is your point of view or is it your awareness of all of the structures and people who would rather die than change. In case you haven't noticed, there are a LOT of people who totally resist change, to the point of preferring that their body dies. Crazy huh? We're back to Goethe and his idea that planet earth is a mental institution for the Universe. How does it get better than this?

The funniest thing about change is that it is not an insane monster. It is not a dragon in disguise. Change brings beauty to living. Change brings the gift of living. Change brings an energy of living that opens the door to all possibilities.

When someone makes you wrong for changing, it usually means you have stopped living the limited life that you both had in common. That means it's time to celebrate! And maybe find some new friends who are willing to support you and have your back!

You can choose change, or you can resist it with every bit of energy you have. If you're tired, I wonder how much resistance of change is present in your life? I had burnout three times. The last time was severe. My short term memory didn't even retain 'Would you like some chocolate?' before I'd have to say 'What did you just say to me?' (Truly! I wish I were joking!)

When I was looking at what created the burnout, every single time it was a resistance to change. A resistance to having a greater life. A resistance to creating something totally different. The resistance to being as different as I am.

The gift of burnout for me was about being booted (not very gently) into a new reality. My reality. And now, I'm not waiting for burnout anymore to choose something different. If I ever wake up and my life is exactly the same as it was yesterday, I'm asking "What can I be, do or create different here?"

Destroying my life because my being is so desperate for change will never happen again. Change is the gift I was asking for, that I was also refusing to unwrap. And the funny thing is… I was a change manager. I was happy to create change everywhere, except in my life. My life was way too small for me. I was possibly the only person who didn't know it!

There are different types of destruction. Some destruction is required for creation to occur. You can also destroy and uncreate what isn't working for you to shatter your old patterns and unleash your energy. Waiting for change without taking action can make you very tired.

So what are you willing to destroy rather than destroying your entire life or business? How many unfinished projects do you have that no longer contribute to you? Sometimes we create as a way of processing and coping with the events of our life. When we move on, we forget to move our projects on too! Letting go of the old projects makes room for the new ideas that can create something even greater. If you make nothing you create significant, then allowing projects to die a natural death can be a gift. We can have ease with change if we are willing to choose it!

Creating From Destruction

When you don't want something in your life anymore you destroy it. I've had clients who have destroyed their businesses because they didn't want to work in it anymore. My dad fell asleep on the highway and rolled his new car to the point where it was a write-off. He walked away without a scratch. We discovered he didn't really want that car. I got burnout so I couldn't go to my ridiculous job anymore. It sounds extreme, and it's almost always unconscious. Don't make yourself wrong for creating insanity. Do ask questions so that you can start the process of change without totally destroying your life.

Anytime something in your life isn't working you have to ask 'Do I still desire to create this?' If it is a 'Hell yes!' (not a reluctant 'oh I should I guess' kind of yes!!) then ask to upgrade your life or business rather than destroy it! If it is a no, then ask what can you change or create that would allow more ease as you transition into a different smorgasbord of choices.

I've also observed people create (or destroy by not creating) from revenge. What do I mean? Well, have you ever seen one partner refuse to work because they think their partner should be working harder or creating more? Have you ever done this and it's worked out wonderfully for both of you? Or did it actually create so much less than either of you desired? Using 'not creating' as a way of punishing someone is a form of passive aggression and it never works.

It also occurs in businesses all the time. People go slow, or they do things wrong, or they don't do the one essential thing that would keep a client happy because they are full of resentment or anger. This is creation through destruction. It is always a choice, but know that it first destroys the person who is hell-bent on creating the destruction. Choosing against someone is not choosing for you. You end up choosing against both of you! Are you enjoying that or is it time to stop creating from a platform of destruction?

It's like being a child and playing Lego. You build something, get bored and then destroy what you've created so you can create all over again. Which is great...

until you wear yourself out by always starting from scratch. What if everything you create could become a platform for building something even greater, rather than a platform for the destruction of your genius? Creating crap is not a wrongness... it's just an interesting choice that we use to stop ourselves from creating something amazing!

And know that there are times when you do need to destroy something to create something even greater. The key is to ask 'If I destroy this, will I (or can I) create something greater?' If the energy expands and gets lighter, find a way to dismantle your creation gracefully so that you can begin the process of creation in a different way. There's no need to suffer throughout the destruction process.

What Are You Asking To Create?

I was having a mighty big whinge to myself one day about how nothing was showing up fast enough or big enough in my life. My level of disgust that the Universe was not on top of my requests was at an all-time high. And then I had this quiet little moment of inspiration. 'I wonder what is it exactly that I'm asking for?' So I made a list. It had 12 things on it. In total. There, on paper, was the evidence of the limitations of my life.

I was shocked. Surely I must be asking for more than that? No. That was it. I stopped complaining about the Universe's slack attitude to my requests and I got busy adding to that list. My target is to be asking for a thousand things. I don't have a point of view that they all have to show up. I just knew that by asking for a thousand things, instead of twelve, my entire life would expand. That was almost five years ago and so much has changed! And I am still asking for more. I add to that list whenever something or someone inspires me. Whenever I have a wild idea that is totally outside of the norm. Whenever my life becomes 'too slow'.

This is my inspiration list for whenever I am beginning to get bored with my life. It's a reminder of the beginning of everything I am asking to create. I have no idea how most of those things will be created, but I'm willing to ask for the possibilities to show up. It's not a bucket list. I'm not obsessed with creating this stuff before I die. Some of it probably won't show up in my lifetime. That isn't relevant. I'm creating for the futures I would love this planet to have.

When you make a request of the Universe you begin a co-creative process. As long as you don't decide 'Well that never showed up, you suck at your job Universe' your creation keeps being created long into the future. Some things I started asking for as a teenager are just starting to show up now. I might have gone on a few detours, but I didn't give up! It is the contribution of our energy that creates our possible futures. You have to stop making it all about only the results you can see. Wanting to prove you can create is the biggest limitation you can place on your creations.

Creating By Request

Are you willing to have a full glass? A full life that is everything you are asking for? Or are you avoiding asking in case what you request does not show up? "Be grateful for what you've got. Shut-up." Ever had anyone say that to you? It's not exactly an invitation to ask for more!

One of the best books I've read in a long time is Amanda Palmer's *The Art of Asking*. It was written after her brilliant TED talk and it is an unconventional exploration of both asking and receiving. If you've never been willing to ask for what you truly desire then 'The Art of Asking' is a great inspiration to ask for anything and everything and then receive the magic that appears.

So often the Universe delivers exactly what we are asking for, but we thought it would be a different colour, so we refuse to receive. I was brought up to be independent. I was not interested in getting married and I did not like the idea of depending on anyone for anything. This resistance to receiving has not been my best choice. As I've become more aware of what fierce independence actually creates, I've made many changes to invite and embrace the gifts that have been offered to me. The Universe always has our back, we just need to be willing to receive it, however it shows up.

****** EXPLORATION ******

What are YOU asking for? Make your list!

Contrary to what you've heard elsewhere, you're not wrong if you don't make your list specific, and you're not wrong if it's general or it doesn't have a time frame attached to each thing. It's not a bucket list. It's not a list of goals. It's a list of creations that would be fun for you! The more you define the list, the less choices the Universe can present to you.

This list is not about creating a set of conclusions about what 'must' show up. When you have a big list of delicious things you are asking for, anything can and will show up. And then you get to choose!

If you are good you will be patient and wait for your list to show up. Or… you could have total choice in every moment if you are asking for a lot of things. What is fun for you? Waiting excludes spontaneity and flexibility. If you are always in 'wait' mode, how creative do you get to be?

Your list is not a prison sentence. It's about constant creation. You are welcome to change your requests at any time! And to choose to receive or not when your requests show up. This is a list of adventures, not a list of targets to be met at any or all cost!

CREATING ISN'T LOGICAL

Osho's wisdom holds true whether we are talking about creating, living or dying: *"We come from the unknown and we go on moving into the unknown."* It is only our irrational mind that wants to know the answer to everything before we choose it!

If I had a dollar for every time someone has said to me "I just want to know the right way to do this so it will be created quickly and easily and it will be super-successful," I'd be sitting pretty on a tropical island, sipping endless Caipirinhas.

Logic is the fantasy we use to keep our comfort bubbles in place. Logic only became more "acceptable" than awareness with the rise of science - and have you noticed how often scientific theories are disproven and replaced? For every 'evidence-based' practice that now exists, there was originally someone who did something new, innovative and (dare I say it) unproven! If we only create based on logic and evidence, evolution will come to a grinding halt.

What is it in life that actually works by logic? Have you seen our governments? Our schools? Our banking systems? The obsession with war? The dominance of big business at the expense of the planet and people's health? There is no logic in any of this, and yet it continues to exist.

Online marketing gurus have presented creating a business as something you can do to a formula or a system. Franchises are based on the idea that if you replicate a system, you'll be successful. It's a beautiful promise, and one that is often broken. When I was a marketing manager for shopping centres I watched many a retailer buy a franchise system and watch their investment disappear because they hadn't made the most important investment of all - an investment in creating themselves as capable business owners. It's what YOU add to the system or formula that creates your success, not the formula or system itself. When did you become a rule-following robot? Would you stop acting like that is fun for you?

If you are creating something magical, something that reflects who you are, something that will make a difference in the world, would you need to put YOU into the equation first? Most systems leave out the most creative element - the people! Most structures try to overcome the shortcomings of people by putting so many rules into place that the people can't get it wrong. Except that the person on the other end of those rules finds them incredibly frustrating. Ever talked to a telco? Or suffered the effects of non-stop telemarketing by a so-called business guru? You know exactly what I'm talking about!

So creating isn't about rules. It's about breaking rules, finding your own way, taking the path less travelled. And if you create your way, you're going to find that creating isn't logical at all. Even the people who think they make choices based on logic may be in for a rude surprise. A few years ago, neuroscientist Antonio Damasio demonstrated that decisions are made emotionally rather than logically. Marketers have known this for a long time. And your awareness will out-create both logic and emotion. What is it you know about this that could change the way you create, if you would allow it?

Are You Willing to BE... Undefined? Unconfined? Unrefined?

Your ideas are great just as they are. You don't need to make them perfect before you start. You just need to start.

The less definition you give your ideas, the greater the possibilities you can invite.

The less refining you do, the fresher and more innovative your ideas will be.

The less confined you make your implementation, the more ease you will have.

The less planning you do, the faster you'll bring your idea into the world.

Questions Create. Conclusions Contract!

I went to the Tate Modern gallery in London. It was quite an education for me in how some artists create. What I saw was various piles of random junk set up in ultra-modern gallery caverns. And with each pile of random junk there was an intellectual discourse full of conclusions about the meaning of the 'artwork'. I was so excited - it made me want to visit the local tip! If creating is that easy, where do I start?

These 'artworks' were not creating a different future; they were not creating questions in the viewer's world; they were simply a way of presenting an intellectual concept. It offered me a different perspective on the contraction of possibilities that is present when we create from conclusions - and I was grateful for that!

I did wonder what difference they could have made if they had created the artworks from a space of question and creating something different in the world, rather than trying to prove a set of conclusions framed by the context of 'it must be good, it's in the Tate'.

Contrast that situation with a stunt pulled by subversive graffiti artist Banksy, who, in 2013, set up a sidewalk art sale in New York. His artwork sells for hundreds of thousands (and even millions) of dollars, and he did an experiment where he sold his images for just $60 each, almost all of them to people who had no idea of his reputation. At the end of the day he had $420. Without context, people did not find his art so valuable. One of the sidewalk artworks later sold at auction for $249,000. It was a funny social experiment, and it shows how many of our creative choices are made based on the context created by other people. So is it real? Or is it just a creation? What could you create that would create unexpected value in the world?

When you create from the energy of questions, you start to create something that is beyond what already exists, beyond the conclusions that lots of people have agreed are real. When you create from your existing conclusions and judgements, it's not easy to go beyond what you already know. Which style of creation would be the most fun for you?

You have been taught to ask questions only if you know the answer or can find it easily. Most managers operate on this principle, leading to people basing their decisions on lots of conclusions that are nothing to do with reality and everything to do with the politics instead of the pragmatics. (Oh my corporate job... how much I don't miss you!)

Asking questions that create more is a creative art. How many questions can you ask in a day? Thousands! And then you begin to create from question, rather than the hundreds of conclusions which limit your creativity.

Creating From The Past

How often have you seen a business owner do their budgets by adding 5-10 percent to everything? Is that creation or is that functioning from the past in a way that has no real relevance to creating the future?

What if everything in the past is totally irrelevant? The last second... irrelevant. What are you choosing right now?

We are great at creating from the past "Last time I did this, that happened" is the habitual conclusion we come to, rather than asking questions. What is different about this situation? What is different about who you are now? What is different about the people involved? What is different about the timing? It's too easy to assume. There is nothing creative about operating from our past assumptions.

Lisa Murray

You may have noticed that many of the greatest inventions are now coming from teenagers. A 19 year-old invented a machine that will remove plastic from the ocean. A 17 year-old American pianist used her awareness of sound waves to invent a new way to detect land-mines. What if age is irrelevant and the past is just the past, not a predictor for the future?

Right Timing

Timing is one of the biggest frustrations for prolific creators! Either you are ahead of your time, your playmates aren't ready to play yet, or you see someone put your idea out just before you do! It can be crazy-making. Or you can ask to work with the timing that is available to you.

Often my ideas are ahead of the mainstream. That is not enough to stop me. Once I become aware that an idea is more than people are ready for, I explore how I can talk about these ideas in ways people can receive right now. And sometimes, the choice that will create the most for the future is to put the ideas aside and wait until there are more possibilities available. There is always a way.

Sometimes I create or write ideas that aren't even a project yet. And this sounds crazy - especially if you have as much going on as I do. Why would I work on something that's not even on the project list? Firstly it gets the ideas out of my head, so I'm less distracted on the other projects. And often I'll begin the creation and then a

STOP WAITING, START CREATING

week or three later, someone will ask for what I've created. And so it's ready to go with just a few tweaks.

That is an awareness of the future, and being willing to have ease with creation. And it's available to all of us if we are willing to create from our awareness rather than our logic! So how do you move your projects into 'right timing'? You ask questions:

What is able to move forward the fastest?
What can move forward with the most ease?
What can I create today that will create the most for today and the future?
What's next? (And go with what pops out at you, not what your logical mind thinks it knows.)

I used to wonder why time management was such a mystery to me, even though I studied some of the best systems out there. I've realised it is because managing time is an invention. You can't manage time. You can manage your energy and attention. You can only direct your energy towards what you would like to create.

If you are aware of possibilities, that can also be the ideas which can move forward the fastest. Not from logic, from awareness of the future.

If you try to control your creative process by saying "I'm only going to focus on _____" (one thing) you stop the timing of everything. Have you noticed? And you then begin to create by force because you have made a decision you are not willing to change.

Once you are in 'creation by force' mode, it's easy to fall into the miseries of 'this isn't working' and 'I can't do this' and 'I'm wrong'. When you create from flow, none of this even enters your Universe! Focus is like being on a highway heading for a tunnel - your vision is limited. Flow is like being on a superhighway as wide as it is long - you are aware of everything.

Focus and force are a contraction of our creative capacities. They limit our awareness to the project in front of us, rather than inviting all of our projects into being in whatever way they can show up.

Following Your Inspiration

If you have inspiration, you don't need motivation. When people describe me as a motivational speaker I get all squidgy and squirmy inside. It doesn't sit well because I know I can't motivate anyone, but I can inspire them to create beyond their supposed limitations. Motivation is an inside job, no-one can give it to you. So stop seeking it outside of you and instead begin to ask for inspiration to show up!

What does inspiration look like?

Your friend who writes to you all worried about the success of a project you are working on together, but then tells you she has gone 40 days without alcohol and is loving it.

The generosity of people who share their knowledge and insights into creating success in that exact moment when you need it.

STOP WAITING, START CREATING

The magic of putting six loosely connected ideas together and coming up with something that has never existed before.

That one word or phrase that gifts you the missing information you have been seeking.

Dinner with friends where you talk about possibilities for changing the world, rather than other people's business.

Meeting a not-so-random stranger that totally changes your life with the gift of their presence!

Being able to improvise when an idea doesn't show up how you imagined.

If you will allow it, inspiration is the whisper that says 'Come here…what you are asking for is this way!' It is that quiet clear knowing that silently leads you into creating with ease. It doesn't have to be the hit over the head with the 2x4! That is only reserved for those times when you consistently ignore the whispers.

Have you embraced your knowing or are you still resisting your awareness in favour of making your creative path as rocky as possible? Being on the creative edge of creation comes when you follow the inklings, the nudges and the cheeky winks from the Universe.

Playing with these 'aha' moments sounds wonderful, until that little voice of doubt pops its ugly head in. "What if I'm wrong? What if it doesn't work? What if the client hates it? What if… blah blah blah…?'

I stopped this kind of 'what if…' head tripping when I asked myself, 'Okay, what is the worst thing that can happen? Will I die? Will I be embarrassed? Will I have to change something? What if none of that is bad? Okay - I'll try it!' The funny thing is, my awareness has proven to be a lot more accurate than my logical mind.

Lisa Murray

There is a different world of 'what ifs....' that is possible. 'What if this could be even more phenomenal than I imagine? What if this could lead somewhere I haven't yet thought of? What if I know way more about this than I've ever acknowledged? What if this is just the start of what's possible?

Following your inspiration is the start of being aware of your creative process. When you have a variety of creative processes to draw on, you won't get stuck. You'll keep moving forward, because that's how you roll.

~SECTION 3~
EXPLORING YOUR CREATIVE PROCESS

NURTURING YOUR CREATIVE PROCESSES

Your creative process isn't a complicated machine. It's the ways you nurture your ideas into the world that allow you to create what you would love to create. We all have creative processes and mostly we use them out of habit, rather than as an expression of who we truly be or as an expansion of what we are truly capable of!

Even as a teenager I had a clear creative process. How do I know this? Everyone would ask 'what are you going to do when you leave school?' and I would respond 'Go to university and do marketing.' The funny thing was, I didn't even know what marketing was, I just knew it would work for me. When the time came, my lack of diligence at school did not get me the university offer I desired. But my demand to have this come to fruition was stronger than that. I did not give up on my dream. I kept asking how else it could become possible, even though it seemed almost impossible.

I started a course at another university, and through family connections, I ended up living on the campus at the university I preferred. Within a week of starting at the other university I got the offer to do a marketing degree at my chosen institution - where I was already living! And it was beautiful, a campus set on a nature reserve, where I did not have to experience the intensity of a big city unless I chose to venture out into the world. While none of this was 'planned' I recognise that I created it and that it was perfect for the quiet, anxious introvert that I was.

Choosing marketing as a career lead me into many years of working with some of the most amazing creators in the world, and being able to be creative in my daily work, for which I am truly grateful! Even as a seventeen year old, I knew how to create exactly what I desired and what would work for me! And it wasn't cognitive. There wasn't a defined 'why' or 'how'. It was a choice to follow what I knew. How many of our choices do we try to justify, rather than going "that's what I am choosing, just because I can!"?

That clarity of choice is one way of inviting your creative process to work for you rather than against you. Every time you second-guess yourself or try to find the reasons for your choice, you stop your creative process mid-creation. What made this particular creation possible was that there was no doubt in my Universe that I would get what I desired. Even when it looked totally different on the outside, I did not waver in my sense of what was possible. That intensity of demand creates magic!

Playing with your creative process is a way to invite a more cognitive sense of what you do naturally. We all create, in every moment of every day. Being aware of your creative processes allows you to create what you truly desire, rather than creating chaos. Your life becomes the adventure of conscious creating, rather than the misadventure of unconscious creating.

I wish I could say that everything has just become more and more amazing since my seventeen year old self discovered that creating was easy. But no, like many people, the more I tried to fit in and get it 'right', the less I used my natural creative processes.

At university I was taught 'the right way' to create a business. Once I was in the workforce I was taught 'the right way' to get on with people and the 'right way' to get promotions (which was mostly to not rock the boat).

Unfortunately 'the right way' was a huge limitation of what I was capable of, and it lead to me creating lots of not so fun things when I could have been creating beautiful, brilliant magic. I wonder if this is true for you too?

Having burnout not once but three times in less than fifteen years of working in corporate environments should have been a huge hint that my creative process had gone missing in action. But I still didn't get it. Fitting in and doing it 'right' had become more valuable to me than my own knowing. I was good at what I did and "there is nothing wrong with me" was the point of view which kept me in creative purgatory.

At the same time, I spent literally years thinking I was a loser because I couldn't create what I desired. That was the lie that was sticking me. The truth is I can create anything, but I was so busy being everything BUT me, that 'not me' couldn't create a damn thing. True story. If you are trying to be who you are not, your creative process will be a red hot sticky mess of confusion and it probably isn't working for you. You can't create from energies or spaces that are not truly you! (That's just one more reason why it's so not a good idea to copy other people!)

Lisa Murray

It was only when I made a new demand of myself to be 100000000000000000% ME that I could begin to discover how my personal creative process works. And now, anytime a project isn't working how I would like, I ask "Where am I not being ME in here?" The awareness comes very quickly! Literally, if I'm cranky or frustrated, I'm not being me. I don't have to guess!

Over the last few years I've talked to thousands of people about their creative process. It's fascinating to me how many people are still desiring to copy my creative process. They ask me questions on 'how' I create, in the hope that they'll uncover the magic recipe that will forever make creating easy for them.

It doesn't work like that. My creative process is ever-changing. It changes for different types of projects. It changes according to how inspired I am in the moment and what I am inspired by. It changes whenever I have a sense of a different possibility. I don't rely on previous ways of creating to create my future adventures.

Writing feeds the creative processes for all of my other projects in so many ways. It is not uncommon for me to wake up, have the idea I'd like to write about, and then realise that everything I know about writing has disappeared. It's a form of the blank. But it's not writer's block. It shows up like this when I've stepped into a new space of 'how I create' and I don't yet have a cognitive sense of it. Sounds weird. Let me tell you... it is! Disconcerting doesn't cover it.

And here is where I'm different to almost everyone I know. I don't make it wrong or bad. I don't assume I have writers block. I just ask: "Is this a new space of creation?" or "Am I leaping into a new way of being with my (writing) capacities?" If the energy expands and gets lighter, I know that I just need to start wherever I can (even if it's badly!), and over the coming days, my new way of being with words will flow. Getting into a creative flow is always simpler than we make it.

This 'quantum leap' energy I've just been describing is part of my creative process. I'm always asking to be aware of any new energies of creation that I can play with, whether I can explain them to others or not, whether I have words for them or not. I don't limit my creative process to what makes sense! How undefined, unconfined and 'unboxable' are you willing to be?

Diving deep into your creative processes also creates expansion of your life. If you apply whatever you learn in creating your ideas and projects to everything, your life will continually expand!

Identifying Your Creative Process

Right now you have a creative process (or many!), whether you acknowledge this or not. Here's a simple way to start being aware of how you create. Get the energy of three truly amazing creations in your life, things that made you go "Wow! How did that happen?" and then ask yourself the selfie-interview questions below.

The first thing to know is that these amazing things didn't just 'happen', in some way, you chose them and you created them. If you don't acknowledge this, you will always limit your possibilities for creation. It wasn't synchronicity. It wasn't luck. It wasn't coincidence. If you think that, you'll stop the creations that are possible.

Maybe there's a way through this that will create more for you and the world!

I have a series of interviews on the Creativity Lab Blog where creative people of all kinds talk about their creative process. Almost every time I send the interview questions off, I receive feedback that these questions invite the interviewee to delve deeper into how they create.

I'm offering you the very same questions here. You may not yet know the answers. In asking them, new possibilities for having your creative process expand are invited. You may choose to revisit these questions regularly. I am always surprised how much has changed. (If you'd like to be featured, send me your responses via www.CreativityLab.tv/cpblogfeature)

****** EXPLORATION ******

What's your creative process?

Ask these questions and start to acknowledge how it is that you create. Your process will shift and change as you do and as you create different ideas. There is no right answer to these questions! Have fun! You can also ask the questions once a year - it's a great New Year's Eve adventure... to see how far you've come each year!

1. *What are you currently creating?*
2. *What does being aware of your creative process make possible, that would otherwise be impossible?*

STOP WAITING, START CREATING

3. What is your distinctive creative process... how does it work for you?
4. Where are your play spaces? Where do you most love to create? What makes it work for you?
5. What is the most unusual creation you have invited into the world? What was your role in bringing it to life?
6. What is it about your creative process that is unique to you? (What is it that people go 'wow, I've never seen anyone create like that before?')
7. How do you choose what to create and what to leave in the land of ideas?
8. What is your best tip for finishing (or starting) a new idea?
9. How do you nurture your creativity and your creations?
10. What inspires you to create?
11. What do you desire to change in the world through your creations?
12. What's your most phenomenal 'I created...' story?
13. What kind of 'impossible' future are you creating? How are you starting?
14. Which of your gifts and talents did you value the least and what changed with your creative process when you started exploring it?
15. What has your creative process allowed you to achieve that would not have been possible otherwise?

Lisa Murray

Discovering You Are Creative

Are you reading this thinking "I have no idea where to start! Those questions are like a foreign language to me. Maybe I need to do a course or something!" Well, I hear you. This was where I started when I had burnout. I had no idea what I enjoyed doing. My creative spark was buried deep, and the burnout was the earthquake that triggered the volcano of creation that I've been playing with ever since!

After spending thousands of dollars on physical treatments with very little result, I realised my burnout was not so much caused by a physical issue (although it was showing up like that) as the miserable situation of my creative energies having had the life suffocated out of them. When I began the process of rediscovering my creative capacities everything began changing with my body. It never shows up how you think it will!

I started being more creative by making a list of things I enjoyed. There were about five things on that list in the beginning. Not exactly the impressive and awe-inspiring start I was hoping for. Then I stumbled across Julia Cameron's "The Artists Way" book, which lead me to start writing and taking myself on fun adventures once a week. From these tiny choices, much bigger discoveries became possible.

You have to start where you are. Go places you haven't been. Have adventures you haven't had before. Embracing the new is one of the greatest inspirations

STOP WAITING, START CREATING

available to us. If you were curious about EVERYTHING, how could your creative process expand? Now, whatever magic I discover, I always ask, "what's beyond this?" There is no end to what's possible once you start!

In my coaching I've often seen clients think they need to learn something from someone else rather than having the adventure of discovering what they know and how their individual approach to creating can add to what is known in the world.

If you think that another course will create the magic you are asking for, you have to ask yourself "If I do this course, will it create what I'm truly asking for?" Don't go on the logic, go to the energy of what is possible if you and the course make love. No workshop can give you the answer... it's what you bring to the workshop that creates the magic. Are you willing to give it the magic that is you? Without limits? Without making yourself less than the teacher or facilitator? In that space, your creative processes can expand. What do YOU know?

The other thing is, I rarely finish the courses I take. And I don't make myself wrong for that! The target isn't to finish, the target is to discover something new. I once had a boss who would send me to a conference as long as I was sure I'd learn at least one new cool amazing thing that we could implement. His view was that the time and cost was worth it. (Yes, he was a fabulous boss - one of the best and I am still so grateful for everything he taught me.)

Before I sign-up for any kind of learning experience (creative or business-related), I ask "If I choose this, will it expand my life and business?" If it is a yes, then I ask "Which parts of this are relevant to me?" and "How do I apply this information or insight to create something even more phenomenal than what I have now?" It is these questions which create the greatest value for me. I'm not expecting anyone else to show me my creative possibilities.

Nurturing your creative process is a life-long adventure, not a target to tick off your to-do list. If you allow it, it will weave its way through your world in the most delightful and surprising ways. You'll discover hidden talents and gifts. Your brilliance will begin emerging into the world in unexpected ways. This is a journey to be savoured rather than slurped.

MULTIPLE PROJECTS – THE NEW MULTI-TASKING

In the 1990s, multi-tasking was hailed as the answer to productivity. "Juggle more things, faster" was how you were expected to get through your unbearable workload. Multi-tasking became the gold-plated invitation to activating your previously well-hidden ADHD tendencies.

Studies have since shown that multi-tasking as a productivity tool is nothing but a myth that makes us feel bad because we feel like we're constantly going round in circles and nothing is completed.

If the title of this book had you at "Stop Waiting", the first question to ask yourself is how many projects do you have going on? Less than five? Between five and ten? More than ten? More than twenty? More than fifty?

Most people who have more than five projects on the go judge themselves as having too many projects. We've been told to focus. What if the opposite is true? What if you don't have enough going on to keep you creating prolifically? I used to choose my jobs based on how many different projects I would be able to play with at once. The jobs I hated the most were the ones where a routine was expected of me, where I had to fit my creative capacities to the limited resources available, where I was only allowed to have a couple of things going on. The jobs I loved (and where I was most loved) were those where there were many ideas and projects being created non-stop. When I applied this approach to my life, everything became way more fun!!

Having multiple projects going on is a way into greater creative productivity. When you have multiple projects your creative muse can visit way more often. The new multi-tasking is not about doing everything at once or trying to juggle everything without dropping anything. It's about having so much choice in your projects so that there is always something moving forward with ease. Big difference!!

How? Consider the difference between having three projects going on and having thirty projects going on. Just for a moment, put aside the overwhelm, and look at the possibilities.

What are the chances you'll be inspired by one or more of your three projects for eight hours a day? It's possible... and there are going to be a lot of days where you just don't feel like creating anything!

What are the chances you'll be inspired by one or more of your thirty projects for eight hours a day? Most likely you'll be happy playing with your projects for way more than eight hours a day!

I have around 30 – 50 projects going at any one time. And I play with the one that 'pops' when I ask 'What's next?' I keep creating and expanding that project until I'm bored or have run out of ideas. Then I ask 'What's next?' and I repeat the process. I could play with a project for 5 minutes or five hours. The amount of time is irrelevant. What's important is that I keep a creative flow going. At the end of any given day, there is plenty of progress. This is how you give your creative muse a full-time job!

So let's talk about why you are avoiding having multiple projects going on.

Not Enough Ideas (Or No Ideas!)

If your creative platter is empty, and your flow of ideas is at a complete standstill, the first questions to ask are "What am I unwilling to know?" and "What am I unwilling to be?"

We all have ideas. Some of us have just become experts at squashing them into non-existence. I was a perfect example of this. Over twenty years of corporate cubicles and non-stop judgement had turned my right brain into mushy peas. There was a little excavating required!

If you think you have no ideas, take one thing you would love to be different in the world. And begin to create ideas around what could be changed. Research. Talk to people. Ask the crazy questions that no-one is willing to ask. Get curious about what would be counter-intuitive to most. Is it? Dream the impossible dreams. Make a request of the Universe. And write down every skerrick of an idea that shows up. It's amazing how these sweet things go on to have idea babies as your future evolves! Some of them even become money babies too!

Lisa Murray

Make it your target to come up with at least fifty ideas on creating this change. You don't have to implement any of them, you just need to build your idea muscle! And of course, if there is an idea or three that you fall in love with, there's nothing stopping you from starting to create.

One of my favourite books is 'Illusions' by Richard Bach. In it, there is an ideas foundry where all ideas are 'manufactured' by idea fairies. It made me realise there are literally trillions of ideas floating in the ethers, and it's our choice if we play with them or not. If we choose not to, we can't complain when someone else brings our ideas into reality.

Ideas are oneness in action, a demonstration that we are all so much more connected than we imagine. How many ideas have you had, that you didn't do anything with? Did someone create your idea and then you spent the next little while beating yourself up for not taking action?

Is it true you have no ideas? Or are you judging the ideas you have into oblivion? (If so, please go explore the 'What If… You're Not Wrong?' chapter in Section 1!) Judgement is a great way to prove to yourself that you can't create anything valuable. Is it making you happy? Wealthy? Free? Or just annoyed with yourself. The cool thing is, YOU are the one who can change this!

STOP WAITING, START CREATING

Overwhelm

Overwhelm shows up when we put pressure on ourselves, when we fail to meet our own expectations or deadlines, when we don't have the required information to make a choice. Many of my business coaching clients come to me with overwhelm. They don't know where to start and they are desperately trying to make 'the right choice'.

I know this is going to be disappointing (especially for the perfectionists and over-achievers) but there is no such thing as a 'right' choice. There is just choice. And every choice is good for ten seconds. No more. If you make a mess, you can clean it up... or just move on. If you make a 'mistake' you can discover something new.

If you create a huge fuck-up, you can embrace the gifts and make some money teaching others about the other choices you've since discovered. Yes, I'm speaking from experience here. Don't waste time with regret. Make money from your temporary stupidity! There are no 'wrong' choices. There are just choices. As Gary Douglas, the founder of Access Consciousness says: "Choice creates awareness."

If you were never wrong, could you truly be overwhelmed? Or could you just be enjoying a party full of choice. As children, we rebel because we perceive we don't have enough choice. As teenagers we assert our choices diligently, pushing boundaries and exploring possibilities. As adults, the pressures of life ensure we quickly forget we have the freedom of choice, finding 'safety' in mimicking the choices of those around us. Is that enough for you? Or is your creative muse desperately trying to show you something totally different?

Overwhelm is a choice. Flow is a choice. Which one would you like to choose?

Overwhelm is often just a lot of information. You can ask 'which information is relevant here?' to find a space to start. My brain works like a library. When I was writing my first book manuscript, I found myself wanting to put in every tiny bit of information. Let's just say it needs a lot of editing! You don't have to give your audience everything, you just need to give them what they require. Often the gap between these two things is huge! It's the same with your ideas! In the tech world they call it creating your minimum viable product. Amazing businesses have been built by astute choices about what to leave out.

The best way to move beyond overwhelm is to start somewhere. To make a choice and move forward with whatever you can.

Make 'move forward, not right' your mantra!

There is another kind of overwhelm you'll often face once you have a lot of projects going on. The sense of everything needing to be done at once. If every project is pulling at you, how do you manage your time?

'What time management system do you use?' is a common question I hear at my events and on telecalls. People are surprised when I say I gave up on time management a long time ago, as I realised it just didn't

STOP WAITING, START CREATING

work for me. Think about it for a moment, you can't manage time, you can only manage your choices. And 'managing' is such a poor description of the choices we truly have available.

Most people perceive time as a series of deadlines or dates of significance. It is a way of measuring change, of judging if we have succeeded against some kind of self-imposed timeframe. When you look at it like this, you can see that 'time' does not create. In truth it is YOU that creates. What if there is another possibility... and it is NOW!?

Albert Einstein's theories of relativity suggest that all moments are equally real. It has also been suggested that time is an illusion, an invention or an idea (literally a creation). We all have these ideas about how long something 'should' take. And I always knew that it didn't take me that long. When I was 21 I briefly worked for my uncle while his secretary was away. At the end of the first morning I'd done everything he gave me. He was confused. Normally it took her most of the week to do those activities. That was one of my first experiences of realising that if we don't define how time works, we can out-create how it is supposed to work! I tried for a long time to 'fit in' to how you 'should' organise your time. And it just never worked for me. So I became unconventional in my approaches and this allows me to create so much more than most people. What if you are way faster than you've allowed yourself to know?

Gary Douglas suggests that we create from space, not time. So now I just ask "What energy, space and consciousness can I and my body be to create this super-fast and with total ease?" When you take time out of the equation of creating, so much more becomes possible. You

Lisa Murray

get into the energy of flow, and you can ask which project is the priority, rather than rolling around in a sea of hogwash that is populated by other people's opinions (or guilt-trips) of what you 'should' do next.

My projects tell me what to work on next. When to start, and when to move onto something else. You may be wondering how they talk to me? I know to start something when it is continually present in my awareness. Or when it just feels like the most fun thing I could choose to play with. I know to change something when I'm bored, when my body gets restless, when I am continually distracting myself, when all I can think about is food (and I know I'm not hungry!).

What is amazing is that when one project goes quiet, another one or two pop into my awareness. There doesn't have to be downtime unless I choose it! If you have a lot of projects, you don't have to create them all at once, unless that's fun for you! Getting into the flow and allowing timing rather than time to be the priority allows overwhelm to totally go away!

If you would like to know more about communicating energetically with your projects, get the free e-class at www.CreativityLab.tv/alchemy.

STOP WAITING, START CREATING

Too Many Ideas - No Idea Where To Start?

When you have a lot of ideas, where do you start? What do you finish first? Where will you be most nourished, nurtured and fulfilled? How do you stay present with the vast amount of possibilities available and still create with ease? Here's how I start...

Make a list of all your ideas. Ask each idea these questions:

◆ *Are you mine to create or shall I leave you for someone else?*

◆ *Is it your time yet? This question will move at least half of your choices into the future.*

◆ *Which one of you will make the biggest difference in the world if I create you now?*

◆ *Which one of you would be the most ease and joy to create right now?*

◆ *Which one of you can I create the fastest today?*

Now take your three ideas that have the most energy, based on the questions above. Which one would you most love to create? Which one would give you the greatest satisfaction if you birthed it into the world? Which one is most insistently demanding to be created? Which one would be the most fun?

I started writing this book because it was pulling me so intensively I could barely think of anything else! As soon as I chose to start writing, quite magically, a clear week appeared in my travel schedule and a friend offered me a beautiful house in the English countryside where I could write. I set a word target for each day and wrote 60% of the book in that first week! What if you would let your projects choose you, rather than being a control freak of magnitude?

Nothing Ever Gets Completed

It's easy to end up with hundreds of incomplete ideas and projects. You just keep starting and you never finish anything. I tried that - it was not my brightest move and it kept me from having a lot of the income streams that now make my business a daily pleasure. Do you know how much fun it is to wake up to unexpected emails about incoming payments from Paypal? It's like a drug for finishing things! Weirdly enough, I'm not especially motivated by money, but I do love the choices it creates.

I now have a simple rule. In any given month, I complete one project that is income producing - and I launch it! If I am not on track to do that, then I will rarely to choose start new projects. No matter how loudly they are whispering my name. I call it blisscipline™. When you choose to create what will generate your life and your

STOP WAITING, START CREATING

business, you choose for you, not against you. There is no how. You just choose to operate from beyond the excuses you tell yourself!

In the words of the brilliant Seth Godin, I also have the satisfaction of 'shipping' every month!

Another element of blisscipline™ is having a 'To-Create' list, rather than a 'To-Do' list. If I had to discipline myself to focus on ticking off a daily 'To-Do' list, creating would get old and boring really quickly! To-do lists are mostly about force rather than flow. A 'To-Create' list is an invitation to play, to explore and to work with the projects that can create the most with the most ease in any given moment.

It's easy to fall into the 'To-Do' doldrums when you have deadlines. The funny thing is, most deadlines are not deadlines at all. You actually won't die if these tasks are not completed. Deadline based 'To-Dos' are a self-imposed way of forcing yourself to work or create. Sometimes it is convenient to agree on timelines so that your creations can move forward, especially when other people are involved. When you have a timeline you have choices throughout the entire timeline - to create or not to create. It is only in the moment you make it a deadline rather than a choice that the bliss disappears!

If you didn't make yourself wrong for not meeting a deadline, what else could be possible? So many times I have not kept to a deadline, only to find out the work was no longer required, the brief had changed, there was a better way to create the outcome, or there was more information available which made the creation process far more ease. If you are 'procrastinating' please ask questions. You may be aware of a totally different possibility that is about to emerge. And you might get to do a whole lot less work than you expected and still create something far greater.

If procrastination was just one step in the flight of stairs that is taking you where you'd most like to go, would you just freaking step over it and keep going? Or would you stay on that step, waiting until all obstacles were removed?

Whatever we resist stops us from receiving more. In 2015 I did a month long personal #Finishathon - it was a creative blitz on getting things finished. It freed up so much energy, so much time, I received so much more money and everything began to flow even more smoothly. What ease are you refusing by not finishing? If you don't know which project to finish first, I have a simple system for making a choice. You can download the free template at www.CreativityLab.tv/Finish. What if finishing things could be fun? (There's more about finishing in the "The Hedonism of Finishing" chapter.)

Blisscipline™ adds ease to my businesses. It adds choice in the moment. It stops me from being bored by routines. And it works with the Universe. When you are creating in flow with the timing of the Universe, everything you desire is created with ease. When you are trying to create ideas that are before their time or not for you to create, you are forcing outcomes... and working way harder than necessary!

STOP WAITING, START CREATING

Simplify to Amplify

I love simplicity... and it's not a natural state for me... I'm messy. I have 10,000 projects going on at once in my head. I have a tendency to over-commit myself because everything sounds so exciting... I'd call myself a recovering 'Queen of Busy'.

Recovering? I know... sounds like I'm lining up to invite you to a 12-step program. No! That would be far too boring! However, making the chaos simple allows you to amplify the change that is truly possible.

When you remove everything that is not required, you receive the clarity that allows you to amplify that which truly makes a difference - to your life, your projects and your business.

Creative Delegation

Do you reach out for help? What I know is... if you are mostly super-amazing (and YOU are!) then people will not offer to help - they think you have it all going on. Are you willing to ask for support and then receive it? You are welcome to join us in the Creativity Lab Facebook Group if you'd like to find other beautiful creators who can contribute to what you're creating.

Oh yeah... one more thing. Remember to say NO when you need to!! Not everything requires a yes so that you can procrastinate for a while before you eventually and reluctantly delegate it at the very last minute.

Lisa Murray

Give Yourself Space to Breathe. Stretch. Connect with the Earth. Have Slow Moments.

Sounds simple. Creates mega-ease quickly. When we ask for energy from the earth and the universe, we get revitalized effortlessly. Your body likes to move. Don't tie it to a desk all day. Go outside, talk to the birds. Explore more ways to receive the space of inspiration.

When we slow down temporarily we get to breathe, acknowledge our creations, and allow the clarity to show up. "What's next?" Space allows you to know what you know - especially the not-so-logical steps. Like which phone calls to answer and which can be for later... When to dip into the biggest ADHD playground in the world (Facebook) and when to power through your work.

Space isn't wrong. Space is the gift that we rarely give ourselves. It nurtures possibilities. When you invite space into your world, your projects receive a different energy of creation. This is where the magic and the miracles show up. Have you noticed that hard work rarely creates in the same way? That's the magic of space.

Create Shortcuts. NOW.

You know when you are really busy and you go 'there must be a faster way to create this!' That is the time to create the shortcut - when you are annoyed and ready to kill. That demand inevitably provides more information about easier ways for moving forward.

It's amazing what shortcuts can be discovered with a little bit of Google love or a request in an online forum where people are willing to contribute to each other! Simplification = speed. Speed = the choice to amplify what's important to YOU.

Power Hours

Do you have a list of 'boring' stuff that is asking for your attention? That maybe you have labelled 'necessary evils' or 'too hard' or something sweet like that? Take that list. Group the like tasks together and give yourself an hour to do as many things as you can, as fast as you can. Make it your target to cross off as many things as possible. Start with the fast, easy items that you have spent more time thinking about than doing. You may be surprised how much creative energy you can free up just by stopping the 'I should…' list that goes through your mind!

And one more thing. Never use your most productive time of day for power hours. I love to write in the mornings. Power hours are for just after lunch or late afternoon, when my creative juices are in their replenishment zones. They are often fuelled with really good chocolate. What do you know about when you are most creative? Is having multiple projects looking like a lot more fun now?

Lisa Murray

Being Creative in Your Routines

If you resist routines as much as I have been known to, there is one possibility that might be fun for you. Being creative in your routines and routinely creative. This way, nothing gets to be boring and you won't ever have to go "Oh no... it's Marketing Monday... ewwwwww." Instead you can get the energy of all of your many projects and go "Hmmm I feel like writing, I wonder which projects need some writing love?" Blocking different projects together under the type of task you feel like doing is a fun way to create!

If you've ever wondered how I can continually be stretching my brand beyond where it has been, being creative in my routines is part of it. There are days I don't feel like working, but I'm happy to enjoy a glass of wine and play with creating images or new brand elements. It doesn't feel like work and it allows the creative expression of my businesses to be continually evolving.

All of these choices create the space to amplify your brilliance. When you simplify, you amplify what can make the greatest difference. How else can you simplify your creative processes?

Are Your Ideas BIG Enough?

If you ever have an idea that you are really excited about, and then you become bored by it quite quickly, chances are the idea isn't big enough for you. Writing one book is boring for me. Writing three at once starts to make it interesting!

When you have multiple projects you can ask all of the projects to contribute to each other. They can have idea babies. And then you can meet other people to collaborate and co-create with and your idea babies can grow up into sexy world-changing ideas that lots of people want to play with.

How many of your projects are related to each other? How can they expand each other? What can you add to each one to make it even greater? These are the questions to ask when you have too many small ideas distracting you from making a difference. What if you are an empire-creator in disguise? Is it time to unhide your ideas and expand them?

Is Having Multiple Projects Still Freaking You Out?

The good news is, you don't have to choose this. You can continue to create in the ways that work for you. I love this way of creating because it speeds everything up. I am rarely bored and there's never a day where I can't move forward. This book was called "Stop Waiting, Start Creating!" for more than one reason!!

DOING & FIXING IS NOT CREATING

"If you would create something, you must be something." ~ **Johann Wolfgang von Goethe**

Business sold us a pack of lies. Somewhere it was decided that our main value is in what we do and what we can fix. What if that is the least of our value? What if that is the least of our creative capacity? What if who we are, what we be and what we are willing to change are so much more valuable than doing and fixing?

These traditional values are inherent in most people's creative process. They are the myths that stop creating from being fun. If you think creating is all about doing and you don't have time to be, or be you, as you create, you'll find creating to be a much harder process than it actually is. If you think creating is all about fixing things, rather than creating new possibilities, you'll always be stuck in a problem-solving mindset. Is that fun for you? Or is that the reason you didn't think you liked creating?

BEing or DOing?

Creation does not come from having enough time or enough talent. It comes from being. Being you. Being space. Being everything you are. Being. When you BE before you DO, you'll create easier, faster and with a greater awareness of exactly what is required.

We are taught to DO first. People ask: "What are you doing today?" I wish they would ask "What are you being today?" or "What are you creating today?" instead. Those conversations would open up the possibilities for so much more to show up.

What do I mean? Well imagine if instead of talking about how busy you are with your 'To-Do' list, you expressed the kindness you would like to bring to the world, the laughter that brightens up your day, the presence that makes people feel alive, the insight that allows you to create with ease... that's the start of being!

Right at this moment you are probably going 'what is BEING?' Before my adventures in creativity, I didn't know either. As a child I learned to create mostly through doing. And then, when I got burnout, that was no longer possible. My body rejected everything connected with doing if it wasn't coming from a space of being. And while I'm long over the exhaustion, there is no faster way to get it back again than to start living in the 'DO DO' world.

And that doesn't mean I didn't try to keep my 'DO DO DO' Universe. I did my best. If it was possible, I'd still

STOP WAITING, START CREATING

have it. Luckily my body is smart and it had other ideas. For the first year after I quit my job, I was still obsessed with doing, even though I could barely lift a finger. Everywhere I went there were flags waving wildly saying 'Just BE'... and I was refusing to listen. My acupuncturist, my massage therapist, random people in the street, psychic friends... they were all saying the same thing. BE.

Why was I resisting this so much? Because I had misinterpreted what being is. I thought it was doing nothing. And actually that is so far from true it makes me sad to see how much pain I put my body through in the pointless pursuit of doing.

Being allows you to create from your presence and your awareness. If there is one energy that out-creates everything, it's presence! Presence comes from being willing to have an intensity of being, and it's different to being present. There are thousands of people with beautiful voices in the world. And a few that are willing to have such a presence that the world sits up and takes notice. Having a gift is more common than we are willing to acknowledge. To create a valuable future with your gifts, you must make the demand to show up!

Here's a fun experiment to play with. Do the washing up or the ironing in your usual (absent-minded) way. Now do it with presence. Do it with all of your awareness present in the moment, rather than being in the future or in the past. Were these two very different experiences? Which one makes you feel more alive? Which one made you feel more 'you'?

Now, the next time you go somewhere, be all of who you are (that's being present), without making yourself smaller or less than the other people there (that's presence!). Did people respond to you in a different way?

Lisa Murray

Did you get better service? More attention? That's the kind of presence we're aiming for! What if you could choose that in every moment? Would your creative capacities expand dynamically?

> *Being present is a way of living consciously.*
> *Having presence is a demand that the world will mould itself to your request.*

Being is not about doing nothing, although that is always a choice! Being is the inspiration you receive when you allow space for ideas to show up and you bring your full presence to the table.

It's the moment in the shower when you solve the thing that has been bugging you for weeks. It's the immersion in nature that allows you to know what YOU know, rather than being confused by the clanging sounds of everyone else's thoughts, feelings and emotions. It's the sense that even though everyone else is going right, you need to go left.

It's having total communion with your pet or your partner - knowing what's up with them without having to talk. It's the tingles your body has when you first dive into the surf on a crisp day or stand on the snow barefoot. It's the razor-sharp awareness you have when you're driving faster than normal or you're on a road you don't know.

Being includes what some people call synchronicity or serendipity in action. It's magic. You BE and what you are asking for shows up because you are present to receive it. It's flow, not force; spontaneity not planning; flexibility and fluidity, not control.

STOP WAITING, START CREATING

When you create from being, your life falls into place with ease. You don't do things that aren't required. You have a knowing that informs your choices. And you know you can change your mind if the energy shifts. Your energy is an invitation to a different possibility. If you are being everything (or everyone!) except you, those magical possibilities get drowned in the noise. You won't hear the whispers unless they get louder and louder and more and more uncomfortable. Burnout was more like a scream for me. What if your being didn't have to scream at you? Would you be willing to have the ease that comes with being first and doing second?

Does this sound way more engaging than hanging around doing nothing? Yes! And if you discover nothing else from this book, except that being is the source of creation and creativity, you'll always be able to create, no matter what your circumstances! Creation doesn't depend on how much money you have. It becomes possible by the magic you be.

The good news is that no-one except you can stop you from being. It doesn't cost anything to be. You don't have to meditate on mountain-tops, turn yourself inside out doing yoga poses or renounce chocolate, wine or sex. You just have to make a choice. To BE first, and allow your DOing to be inspired by your being.

There is no 'how' to being. It's a space you occupy. An energy you be. And you get there by choosing to be you. Dr Dain Heer wrote a wonderful book called "Being You, Changing the World." It's a brilliant introduction to the energies of being if you are curious!

Whenever I am creatively stuck, or something in my business or bank account is not flowing, I ask 'What else would I have to BE for this to change?' It's almost always something I'm not willing to be, rather than something I'm not doing!

A wonderful side-effect of this approach is that when you create from being, you won't be creating problems to fix. You the being isn't that interested in fixing things. You're more interested in creating ideas and projects that are new and fun! Did you know that? Or have you been so immersed in the problem-based reality that we live in that you didn't realise there is another choice? The fun thing is, it is just choice!

Fixing Shit Is Overrated

If you are as crazy as me, you might have once (or twice) put 'problem-solver' on your CV. And you know where that leads? People give you their unsolvable or deeply messed up things to fix, and you don't get to create the brilliance and joy that is possible. That same brilliance that allows you to fix things with ease also creates phenomenal ideas with ease.

Think of the last ten things you did. How many of them were about fixing something? How many of them were about creating something different?

I put a post on Facebook with the hashtag #FixingShitIsOverrated and it polarised people. Some people went to "oh YES! Bring it! I'm so done with fixing shit." Other people were totally defending their right to keep finding and creating shit to fix. The funny thing is, it is all just choice. But if you don't know you have the choice to stop fixing shit, you'll keep doing it.

STOP WAITING, START CREATING

Fixing shit is the dominant paradigm in our reality. My personal point of view is that it's time for change. Here's the thing. My life isn't perfect. But change is not created by fixing shit. The change I am asking for is created by creating new realities. By being more me. By not allowing the shit to get in the way of creating what I truly desire to have. If I was only focused on fixing shit, I wouldn't have found horses to play with, I wouldn't be going overseas multiple times a year, I wouldn't be writing and getting paid for it #FixingShitIsOverrated

If you are going to fix everything before you begin creating, you'll never start. It's a magnificent way to stop you from creating the magic you could create in the world.

I was writing in a cafe and there were two business guys there who talked non-stop for almost three hours about all of the problems they are fixing. They were so proud! It was like a competition to see who was the smartest. They were using their not inconsiderable talents on the least generative and least creative choices available. It was astonishing to me, and then I remembered that this is how most people still do business. (If you would like to create your business in ways that most people think are impossible, check out Business Alchemy Lab at www.BusinessAlchemyLab.com)

Are you using too much of your energy on the least valuable strategy? If you are always seeking challenges that prove your brilliance, you will only see problems. If you are always seeking ideas that can expand your brilliance, you will only see possibilities.

Doing 'fixation' instead of creation is a dinosaur approach. It can only take you backwards. The faster you fix things, the more things will show up to fix! Why? Because the Universe (or your boss!) goes... "Oh! You're great at fixing things... here you go... here's some more! Have a good time with these ones. And let me know when you'd like an even bigger challenge. I've got everything you are asking for!" Can you see where asking for challenges leads? What other choice can you make?

You'll have a lot more fun if you ask to out-create yourself, rather than having a never-ending competition with you or your colleagues to find out what is the hardest problem you can create and then solve! If you must prove your value in the world, do it from the space of creation, not fixation!

So what do you do if you have a problem you just 'have to' fix? Ask these questions:

◆ *'What's beyond this problem?'*

◆ *'If this wasn't a problem to fix, what could it be?'*

◆ *'If this problem didn't exist, what would I choose?'*

◆ *'If I was going to do something different, rather than fix this, what would I choose?'*

◆ *'What choices are available here that can create the most ease?'*

You can fix a problem, or you can create a different possibility than what the world has yet seen. They are two entirely different things. Know which one you are choosing!

What would change if you stopped being oblivious to the possibilities hidden beyond the problems? What would it be like if you started creating ease instead of

STOP WAITING, START CREATING

creating problems? Your value is not in the problems you solve. Your value is in the contribution you are. They are two entirely different things!

I have a darling friend who creates ease wherever she is. Just hanging out with her is ease. Creating with her is ease. Travelling with her is ease. Not talking with her is ease. Talking with her is ease. There is this amazing peace that comes from this ease. Trauma and drama become unnecessary.

To create a different result, you have to ask a different question, make a different choice, explore different possibilities, and sense where your gifts and talents can be a different contribution. How much fun could you have questioning the status quo every time someone presents you with a problem to fix?

And if you'd like to have even more fun, talk about your creative adventures and use the #FixingShitIsOverrated hashtag on social media… you'll have the most surprising conversations! What if we could change the world with one simple choice?

{HOT TIP}

Have you noticed that having fixations makes you sick and tired? And being creative gives you energy? If you've ever been sick and tired of working, just have a look at the balance between fixing and creating… your different possibility starts right there! And if you ever hear yourself saying "I'm sick and tired of…" take notice of the words that follow - that's the space to begin creating change.

CREATING FROM (THE BLANK) SPACE

Writers block. The absence of the muse. Creative blanks. Emotional black holes. Inspiration vacuums. Paralysis. Stagnation. Sucking mediocrity through a straw. No flow. No ideas (or no idea!) The never-ending plateau. Whatever you are calling it, this blank space is much more of a gift than it is presented as.

If you didn't make it wrong, what could it contribute to you? It is only your frenetic demand to be always in a frenzy of creating that makes it 'wrong'. If you let go of the frenzy and the freak-out, you could just enjoy the space! Even if you have a creative deadline looming. Even if you are terrified you might never have a creative idea again.

When you plant flower seeds in the soil, they go through a stage where you can't see them growing. The creative blank is the same. It is only when we misidentify it as something that it's not that we create a problem. If you define your 'deep in the earth' stages as spaces where your creative possibilities aren't growing, you kill them before they can sprout and blossom. Judgement creates the

Lisa Murray

'everything is buried deeper than my excavation equipment can go' energy. What if there is another way?

"And don't think the garden loses its ecstasy in winter. It's quiet, but the roots are down there riotous." ~ **Rumi**

Personally I do not subscribe to the idea of writers block. Or any of the situations described above. What I do know is that there is always something that can be created if we choose, even if it's not the project or idea that we most desire to create. You can't grow tulips in your garden at the height of summer, no matter how hard you try. Go with the seasons of your creations - flow, not force. That blank space is there to contribute to you, not to make you feel incompetent. Invite it. Explore it. And never resist it. When you be present with it, it can become the fertilisation of your inspiration.

If I am in a temporary creation vacuum I cook, without a firm recipe. I invite the random wanderings of my taste-buds to invent new possibilities. It's a different space of creation to writing. It's a way of slipping into a creative space through the back door. Baking is my writing enabler! What's yours?

Creating In The Unknown

Have you ever considered that just by showing up you could be a contribution to someone else's creations? Have you ever imagined that just by asking the question that no-one else is asking, you open doors to a whole new way of being creative for you and other people? If this is not happening for you, go ask other creative people questions about what works for them. It's a way of inviting magic.

Diving deep into new and expansive creative processes is easy if you are willing to let go of what you already know! A beautiful person I know asked me about my writing process. On the surface, it was just a few fairly simple questions and a fun conversation.

In playing with the possibilities with this person I sensed a huge space open up where I could tap into what I truly know about writing. There was so much space that I temporarily lost my sense of this reality. It turned into a funny day - I had literally no idea of how to cross the road, how to read a map or even how to speak coherently.

I could have panicked and shut down all that lovely creative space. After all, it didn't look or feel anything like what I expected. Weird barely covers it!! And yet, this blank, out-of-control space was exactly what I had been asking for. A space for creating from, that went far beyond what's logical.

Most people try to create from a logical, linear place that they can control. What if your creative brilliance lies beyond the edge of what this reality calls normal and appropriate? What if you have to let go of all you know to

Lisa Murray

discover the edges of what you truly know but have not yet put words to?

I once went on a magical mystery tour through the Universe (no drugs needed). I found myself in this huge black space way out in space. I was very surprised to find it was FULL of the energies of creation. There was everything you could imagine there in the 'black hole'. It wasn't empty. Even though I couldn't see a thing, I could sense the subtlety of many different energies being available to contribute to my creations.

When you are faced with a blank page, you can panic, or you can create. When you are sensing 'nothing' it can be nothing, or it can be that your creations have gone for a wander or a wonder through the Universe, collecting all of the energies, contributions and connections required to bring your ideas to life. Just like a dark room is not empty, nor is your page. All you need to do is to tap into the energies that are desiring to contribute to you and ask them to show up with ease.

'Blank' can also be the space we put ourselves into when we don't want to know just how brilliant we are. It's not a cognitive choice, but it's a very effective way to stop yourself! I make the demand of myself to know everything I am hiding with the 'blank' - it's amazing what pops into your awareness when you give the blank some tough love! One of my favourite questions from Access Consciousness founder, Gary Douglas, is "What are you aware of, that you are pretending not to be aware of, that if you would be aware of it, would change everything?" It's a great question for the blank moments. It is surprising what can come when we lower our barriers to knowing.

STOP WAITING, START CREATING

No blank lasts forever. I love Lewis Carroll's version of forever. Alice: "How long is forever?" White Rabbit: "Sometimes just one second."

Conscious creation is an amazing adventure for modern day explorers - and you don't even have to sail off the edge of the world to discover new horizons. Your brilliance is here, now. You change the world by playing with the unknown in unexpected ways. Often it's a process of 'un-becoming' what you are not, that you have been pretending you are, so you can show the world all you truly be.

How do you tap into your creative brilliance? Play! Create for the joy of it, not the outcomes you think you should be creating. Go somewhere you haven't been. Talk to different people. Invite new questions about what you 'know' - and don't assume you know anything!! Imagine futures that have never existed. Your sense of adventure is reflected in the doors you are willing to open. What if something far greater is on the other side? Will you embrace it or ensure that you never leave your comfort bubble? Trust your brilliance... it's taking you somewhere you've been asking to go!

This is how Creativity Lab is created as an ever-changing experiment in Nurturing Ideas Into Life™. Every day is filled with conversations, collaborations, inspirations and spontaneous 'aha' moments where ideas, people and worlds collide to create something that has not been created before. If you are stuck, don't create in a vacuum. Ask to turn up your awareness, receive the gifts and influences of the Universe, add your unique brilliance and turn it all into creative magic.

Lisa Murray

The Most Under-rated Creation Tool Ever!

The award for the Most Under-rated Creation Tool Ever goes to... LISTENING! Why is it under-rated? Well, most people never do it... have you noticed?

What if listening is the secret sauce to creating? I don't mean that surface level 'yes dear' kind of listening. Or the 'repeat back to the person what they said to prove you are listening' kind of listening that you are taught in Interpersonal Skills 101. (That's not listening, that's being a parrot!)

I mean the listening that is barely a whisper. The listening that is so fast that you barely know you've had the idea. The listening that is the universe gently tickling your feet with a feather. The softer it is, the more it tickles!

The listening that silently and intensely begs you to 'stop your busy' and just BE with the idea. The listening that floats by on a summer breeze and teases you with its 'here but not here' presence. This truly is the sound of the universe talking to us.

It's a kind of listening that not many of us know anymore. And yet, it's available to all of us. And if you desire to create something brilliant, it's the kind of listening that delivers what people will call genius.

How do I know about this? I was having an uncertain moment of 'am I sure about this idea?' so I sent a preview of one of my creations to a couple of friends. One of the things they said was how much they loved the name and how much I have a talent for naming things.

Then I had to admit that my projects create themselves... and they name themselves. I just know how to be really good at listening. When you create from this space of supersonic listening, inviting inspiration becomes easy.

And my friends asked to know more about how this listening gig works. So, for YOU too, here are my top 5 tips for listening different.

Have a target bigger than you. Bigger than what you are asking for personally with your life or your business... (For me right now it is inviting the world to the consciousness and awareness that allows ease with change and the creation of new ways of living.)

Ask 'What's missing in the world that I can contribute to creating?' (One of my awarenesses is 'inviting and nurturing change', as most people do change with force or avoidance.)

Ask: 'What do I know about this that I haven't yet acknowledged?' (For me this started with getting clarity with how I create and embracing change - which has always been very different to the norm - I just didn't realise it until now.)

Be willing to change anything and everything as your listening capacities expand. I knew about my new beautiful thing for almost a year before it had a dynamic entry into the world. It started life being known as Creativity Lab Maxi - but when I created it the second time around, the name no longer fitted. If I had forced my creation to fit the original name it would not exist as anything near its full potential. Creativity Lab Maxi turned into The Nurture Project, which has evolved into The Nurture Club. Change creates!

Be willing to start even if you don't know what it is you are creating. Listen deeply throughout the process, without coming to any conclusion about how it is going to turn out. Even as I was making the first webpages for The Nurture Club, I changed a lot of things from what I first imagined the project would be... and I know that even more will change in the future.

When you begin acknowledging your abilities with listening - to the nuances, the undertones, the unspoken, the whispers of the future, the consciousness of everything - rather than pretending you are deaf, dumb and stubbornly doing it 'your way', your capacities for creation will take leaps far into the unknown. And isn't that exactly what you are asking for?

Inviting The Whispers of the Future

Have you ever had a moment of awareness that collided with an awareness you received in the past? I have a lot of awareness of future possibilities. When something shows up that matches any of those energies I begin to ask questions about what can be created. I'm seeking more awareness, not trying to get to the 'right' answer. If I don't have enough clarity, I don't take action until the idea is offering itself to me with ease. It's that being/doing adventure again. In a slightly different way!

Thinking makes you tired. Receiving awareness of what's possible gives you energy. If you write down every idea you have you won't have to use your energy up trying to keep track of your ideas. Or trying to implement them all at once! (That's a kind of manic creation that is just exhausting, as there is way too much force in the timing!) Use your energy to invite your ideas to show up as and when they can!

The whispers of the future show up when we give them space. Space isn't wrong. It's an invitation for future possibilities. Nurture your space. Allow it to be. Invite it to expand. Don't fill your space with regrets of the past or wishes for the future. Your 'If only I could...' wishes and the whispers of the future are two very different things.

What if Focus Is a Limitation?

Many people end up with a creative blank because of focus. Sounds crazy, and yet, I see it all the time. The artist who only plays with one style or one theme. The non-fiction writer who never allows her imagination to contribute. The business owner who is only focused on money and misses out on the bliss and pleasure of creation. Focus is a contraction of our creative capacities. It limits our awareness to the project in front of us. What if you could be aware of every project and every possibility all of the time?

During a speaking presentation, an artist asked me: "What do you do when you are creating prolifically and you still need to manage your home?" She found it difficult to interrupt her work to attend to the washing, or the needs of her family. I asked her: "Do you concentrate only on your project? Or are you aware of everything?"

My approach is to take the awareness of my creations with me, whatever I am doing physically. So I can go do whatever needs to be done, and I'm still present with what I'm creating. I don't lose the tsunami of energy I've been creating with. In reality, I don't ever shut down my creative energy (unless I'm having a meltdown - that's a story for another day). My creative energy is also there when I sleep so I can be creating non-stop. Creating can be energetic as well as physical. Have you ever asked for information before you went to sleep and then when you woke up the information was there? That's creating in your sleep! You've been taught to compartmentalise your life. Is that working for you? What if everything could be just one big creative flow?

When I travel, I'm present with all of my projects, even the ones at home. I do like to finish the sentence when I'm writing, but by including everything in my awareness at once, I can easily interrupt what I'm doing in any moment. I'll know when to call someone, when to go on social media, when something has changed with one of my events or projects, and when I need to ask questions or invite the Universe to send me more information or inspiration.

To me none of it is more important or significant than anything else and so I move between creations quickly and easily. This is what allows the flow and ease of creation to show up every single day!

Your awareness can encompass thousands of things at once. Here's how it works in practice. I'd been asking my friend about where I could get some Thorntons toffees (one of my all-time favourite things!). Some hours later, we were driving through a small village in the English countryside and I spotted a Thorntons sign amongst a hundred other signs. She was amazed that I saw it. I was not. My awareness is always switched on for discovering everything that is relevant to creating joy and ease in my life!

What made me see that sign? Everything has energy. Even toffee! And as soon as that energy was nearby, my body was aware of it and it showed me where to look. Everyone has this capacity, but most people don't want their life to be that easy. Do you?

Work Less. Create More!

We are trained to work hard. To work long hours. To measure our value by our busyness rather than what we create. And this insane approach to work is the cause of burnout, chronic fatigue, exhaustion, breakdowns and a whole lot of other stress-related diseases. Working hard is the most common dis-ease invented and it creates exactly the opposite of what it was designed to do!

We are addicted to work. And the people around us are addicted to work. And if you are not working hard and being 'useful' you are judged to be lazy or not a contribution to society. What if the purpose of life is to enjoy it? Not to work yourself to death!

The crazy thing is, the less I work, the more I create. The more I play, the more I create. When you give yourself space to create, your creative capacities expand. When you fill every waking moment with your 'To-Do' list, your

Lisa Murray

creative capacities contract. Ideas love a void. Inspiration strikes when you allow yourself the gift of space. You know this. Do you get your best ideas at work? Or when you are in the shower, driving, walking on the beach or receiving a great massage?

What if you would be willing to have people think you are lazy, or useless, or good for nothing? When you make yourself immune to their points of view, you get to use your creative energies in the ways that work for you. Whose life are you living? Yours? Or your parents, your kids or your partners? Or maybe even your boss or employers? How is that going for you? Their point of view is not relevant if you know what works for your creative process.

Don't fall into the quagmire of never ending work. It could literally kill you! Work is not valuable. You are valuable. What you create is valuable. Work is not. Work is just one way to create. What if everything you create could be an adventure and an experiment in living joyfully and playfully? If you were valuing you right now, what would you choose?

If you were to 'work' easy, what would be different? If you ruled the world, what would work be like? It's only in the last couple of hundred years (since the industrial and technological revolutions) that society has become obsessed with work and being productive. Before that we communed with nature, we created for the joy of it, we had ways of enhancing our creative energies every day.

STOP WAITING, START CREATING

Hanging Out In Nature

There's a really fast way to have the space that creates. Go hangout in nature, preferably by yourself. When I say hangout, I mean it. Not a brisk walk through a twenty metre path, but an immersion. Be with the trees. Talk with the birds. Feel the ocean moving on your skin. Soak up the sun. Float through the pelting rain as it massages your skin. Place your bare feet on the earth. Touch the flowers, the bark, the grass. For at least an hour or three! And if you can't find the time, use your lunch hour, or hold 'walking meetings' in a local park.

It's another way of being. When you create from this space, everything is different. Your anxiety goes away. You become present with you and your creations. Nature doesn't judge us. It desires to contribute to all that we be.

For a few months, we had a willy wag-tail who came to play every day. If I went for a walk in the garden, he was a skip and a hop behind me. If I sat still, he would climb up my back, across my feet or cheekily nip my fingers. If I was on the computer for too long, he did fly-bys back and forth past my window so that I would come outside. He was a delight to play with and after a few minutes of interaction my capacity to create was refreshed. All of nature would love to contribute to us like this. It is only our blindness to what is possible that stops us receiving it!

Nature creates space - in our body, in our being and in our Universe. And we don't need to be in nature to receive that kind of space either. I once did a meditation walk in

243

the bush, which surprisingly to me, had the same energy as being on the beach. When we are willing to receive without judgement, all energies are available to us, wherever we are. I can now be in big cities, and enjoy the space, ease and peace that I have in nature. This is the magic of creation. Are you willing to change your reality to work in the ways you would love your life to be?

Creating In The Wee Hours

My favourite time to create is between around 2am and 5am. Almost no-one is awake. There is silence, peace and a huge space of creation opens up. I get more done in those hours than the rest of the day. Why? Because all the busy brains are asleep!

One of the most amazing tools I have received from Access Consciousness® is the awareness that most of what we are aware of does not belong to us. We are literally psychic, whether we acknowledge it or not (and it gets way easier when we acknowledge it.)

I found this a bit weird until I spent a weekend way out in the bush. My mind was still and full of space. It was beautiful! And as we drove home towards the city, I could perceive it filling up and getting busier and busier. Another day I was in the traffic and obsessively thinking about ice-cream. Which was ridiculous because at the time I was not especially fond of it. Once I turned in a different direction, all of the ice-cream thoughts melted away.

From these very obvious examples, it became clear to me that virtually no thoughts are mine! If you'd like to clear this space wherever you are, for every thought,

STOP WAITING, START CREATING

feeling or emotion, just ask "Is this mine?" and if you get more space, ask to return it to sender. If you do this nonstop for three days, your entire reality will change. You will not have to be constantly thinking, or being upset by everything occurring in the world, or having feelings that are so intense that you get stuck in them!! You'll begin to have the choice to create from your reality, not the expectations of the rest of the world.

So when I create in the early hours, I'm creating from the space of who I be, not the jumble of the rest of the worlds thoughts, feelings and emotions. I'm always happy at that time too. Surprise! If I get up early, I wake up to my reality, not the reality of the rest of the world. It's truly a beautiful way to start the day.

One last thing. Most tortured artists allow the energies of this reality to torture them into creating. Or they use the energies of depression and unhappiness as their motivation. Would you prefer the space of creation or the torture of creation? It truly is just a choice.

Most depression is a repression of the brilliance you are. Most unhappiness is due to not being willing to choose what would make you happy. If you can't find your way out of these spaces by yourself, find an Access Bars® practitioner. This kind of nurturing touch can change your entire reality. And it's way better than drugs for being able to enjoy your life again.

Find out more at www.bars.accessconsciousness.com. I know people who have not carried out their planned suicides because they got their Bars run and it changed their entire life. Please don't suffer. Your creative genius is worth far more than that!

CONNECTION, COLLABORATION & CO-CREATION

By the standard definitions, I am an introvert. I get my energy from being alone. For most of my life I avoided people as much as possible. I was so aware of their world that it made my world very loud, intense and not so enjoyable. The cool thing is, anything can change if we are willing. I went from being an introvert who took friends to networking events because the events freaked me out, to travelling the world with Creativity Lab through the connections I have made with people online and off! From crying in airports because the intensity of noise, emotion and people was just too much, to running seven classes in five countries in ten days with quite a lot of ease. (Yes, that was a lot of flights - I may not choose that ever again!!!)

So much has changed. And while I still get my energy from solitude and quiet, my ever-expanding life continues to show me how much labels and definitions only matter as much as we allow them to. What labels and definitions

Lisa Murray

have you decided you have to keep forever instead of changing them so you can create anything you damn well choose? Would you give them all up now?

In the beginning I used to invite people to collaborate and co-create on my projects because I thought I had to fill the gaps. That there was something missing. That I wasn't good enough. And then I would find that they wouldn't deliver, so I'd end up doing the thing I thought I couldn't do. It became a bit of a joke with myself. After a few rounds of doing most of the work I realised this was not a good way to create project partnerships!

None of those collaborations worked well because I made myself 'less-than' the other people. I made my awareness and intuition less relevant than theirs. Instead of being the creator and visionary that I am, I based my choices on other people's perspectives. Not my brightest move! And I am so grateful for each and every one of them. Without them, I may never have started, and I wouldn't be creating what I'm creating now!

If we didn't come from a space of lack, we could choose project partners and collaborators based on their brilliance, on their capacity to add something beyond what either of us can do individually.

After quite a lot of self-reflection and using the Access Consciousness® tools and processes, I have come to a space where I know what I bring to the collaboration, and I am willing to receive the awareness of what the other people can bring. I don't need to control them so it is 'done right' and I don't need to make them better than me. At last!! This is a very different energy to creating from the space of 'neither of us are enough to do this, but together we'll manage it somehow'.

STOP WAITING, START CREATING

As I become clearer about my contributions and requirements, the people who show up to collaborate and contribute to my projects also offer more. So it becomes more + more = even more is created! Rather than less + less = less than what's possible.

Connections

If you are a natural connector who will talk to anyone about anything, you may be tempted to skip this section. Please don't! This is a very different approach to connecting that could add even more magic to your brilliant skills! And if you are an introvert who isn't so excited about connecting, you're about to discover a whole new way of being in the world!

I am not one for small talk. To make meeting people not quite as excruciating, I started to play with ways of connecting that could be fun for me. Talking to an audience of one wasn't really going to work for the plans I have for changing the world!! When I went to a live-in conference in Costa Rica a couple of years ago, I made the demand that this had to change, so I did a little experiment.

I asked: "What would it take for me to get really good at being willing to talk to people?" Every single day during that 7-day event, I made it my target to talk to a minimum of five different people that I had not met before, from a space of curiosity and spontaneity. I would look around the room and ask myself "Who would I love to meet right now?" and then I'd go talk to them. It wasn't easy for the first couple of days but I was clear that I was making a demand of myself to be more in the world. That was more important to me than sitting in my comfort bubble. You have to move out of your comfort bubble if you'd like to create a different result!

It was really cool and amazing to see all of the different connections and contributions that showed up. I made some great friendships that wouldn't have happened if I was still stuck in that space of "Leave-Me-ALONE-I-don't-like-talking-to-people". The weird thing was, that was a really fun adventure for me. I had so many wonderful conversations with lots of beautiful people! That event was a turning point for me. Making that choice changed ME so my business could grow dynamically. I've become so good at this connecting thing that I've had clients pay me for contributing these energies to their projects! It truly never shows up how you think it will!

If you be YOU when you talk to people (rather than just an empty shell pretending to be you), and you be present with them, you are being a gift that few people get to receive. When was the last time someone truly listened to you? We are all interconnected. There is a communion with life that is deep within the cellular memory of each and every one of us. If you lower your barriers, drop your protection mechanisms and simply be present with the beautiful being in front of you, I wonder what could change - for you and the world?

I have also discovered that when I'm truly being me I enjoy people! My mother is not especially social and I had adopted a few of her points of view and bought them as mine. As children, we don't differentiate between what is our point of view and what belongs to our parents. If you examine every point of view you have, you might be surprised at what is true for YOU! What points of view

STOP WAITING, START CREATING

have you bought about your social skills, about being an introvert or extrovert, about talking to strangers or about what people think of you that are simply not true? What else would YOU like to choose instead?

So let's talk parties... or family gatherings, conferences, anywhere that lots of people meet. How can an introvert show up with ease? I simply ask questions before I go:

◆ *If I go to this event, what will it create?*

◆ *Who can I contribute to at this event?*

◆ *Who can be a contribution to me at this event?*

◆ *What other possibilities can be created that I haven't yet imagined?*

◆ *What could I be or do differently that would allow me to have a great time here?*

◆ *What would it take to meet people who are interesting to me?*

And of course, if you love to put the cat amongst the canaries, your questions could be more like this:

◆ *Whose Universe can I change beyond all recognition at this event?*

◆ *Where can I make the greatest difference?*

Lisa Murray

◈ *Who can I make the greatest difference with?*
◈ *What would it take for me to be a leader at this event? (Even if no-one follows!)*
◈ *What energy could I be that would move people out of their habitual responses and topics?*
◈ *What can I talk about that would be controversial or fun for me?*

In asking these questions, I'm not looking for an answer. I'm opening up an energy of possibility and playfulness that will allow me to have a good time once I get there. Once I arrive, I seek out the people that have a sense of lightness and expansion, where there is an openness to a different possibility. Just asking 'Who can I talk to next?' allows my awareness to pop in such a way that I can move from one person to another with ease. If you have been very present with the person you are talking to, it is easy to let them know that you need to talk to a couple of other people too, without them feeling like you are dumping them! Be kind - to you and them. You'll know when it is time to move into another conversation, or draw someone else into the conversation so you can leave with ease.

Social media is also a great place to connect. And when I'm there, I am often connecting people together. That's what makes it social! The bigger and more active

STOP WAITING, START CREATING

your network, the greater the contribution you can be, if you're willing to know who is who in the zoo! What if every time you go on social media, instead of complaining about how boring it is, or how much junk you have to sift through, you make the choice to contribute to three people who are adding value to the world? Or contribute to adding value to the online world by being you in unexpected ways. I wonder what that would create for your future?

How do you contribute? By strategically connecting people, by tagging people when there is something going on that could be of interest to them, by offering your insights in ways that invite people to different choices, by engaging with people in unexpected ways.

How do you get over social media overwhelm? Follow the energy. I have a sense of a slight 'tug' of energy when there is a contribution available for me to be. And then I make a choice about when I'm finished - usually I get bored or the energy of possibilities stops. And there are some days where it is all just too much. Where the world is wired and crazy. Those are the days you go out in nature instead! Remember how I talked about us being all connected? When you are online, you are connected with all of those people too. Far more than you realise. Close your computer, step away and go enjoy the sunshine, the rain, or the snow!!

I did a free Access Consciousness® live stream class on "Using Social Media To Your Advantage" that has some fun clearings in it too. You can find it easily at www.CreativityLab.tv/AccessConsciousness

You are also invited to join the private Creativity Lab Facebook group which is free and you'll be part of a community of playful, joyful creators who are creating different possibilities in the world.

https://www.facebook.com/groups/CreativityLabLive/

Who can you connect with? It's a beautiful international community with an energy of inclusion and contribution.

I am living proof you don't have to be a non-stop talker to be a great connector. Strategic connecting is easier for me than an 'anyone, anytime' approach. I am great at knowing exactly who needs to meet who for magic to show up. I use my awareness when I create connections. Often I connect people without even knowing why I am connecting them. I just know they need to meet. When you approach creating connections from this space, possibilities become available which did not exist before. Awareness of what can work for you is where the magic of creation starts! What kind of connecting are you great at? Play with that!!! Use your difference to your advantage.

Collaborations & Co-Creations

I was once invited to an event to create new possibilities for spiritual entrepreneurs. The initiators of the event gave a lovely talk about collaboration and how we were all invited to collaborate with them in this venture… and then proceeded to outline the entire project in minute detail.

STOP WAITING, START CREATING

They had spent a year working on the idea, with no invitations to anyone to collaborate and then they expected the thirty or so people in attendance to contribute their time, resources and energy for free to build this new utopian ideal they had come up with. There was an expectant phone call to see how much time and energy we would contribute for free, and not surprisingly, there was no second meeting. It was an almost instant crash and burn because no-one felt that their contributions would be included or valued. We all have dreams. Bringing people with you requires more than a meeting when you do all the talking. It requires more than being a micro-manager. It requires generosity of spirit in a thousand tiny ways.

If you would love to collaborate with people, you have to leave the doors open for their creative contributions. You cannot be the control freak of magnitude and still expect their contribution. Pharrell Williams put it very succinctly:

"Collaborate with people you can learn from."

Collaboration is about working together towards a common target; co-creation adds creativity and the energy of contribution into the collaborative mix! These strategies can be an incredible gift or an insane drain.

Lisa Murray

"The more I can make a person comfortable in their environment by taking my ego's hat off and leaving it at the door, then they can dive deep within themselves and we can pull out something interesting that people have never heard before. It's the stuff that no one's ever heard before that is really interesting." ~ **Pharrell Williams**

So, how do you engage people in your creations? You ask what they know or would like to know. Every Creativity Lab event is different because of the people that attend. Their questions and requests create the content topics, the adventures we can go on and the possibilities for the future. This book has been created from a collaborative space. I'm grateful to the people who came to the live classes, for the many lively discussions on Facebook and the questions people ask me in their coaching sessions, and of course, the funny adventures I have personally along the way. This wild mix has created the content. I am the writer - and there has been much co-creation in informal ways!

Many of us love to create on our lonesome. And yet, some of the most amazing ideas in the world come out of co-creative collaborations. I am always asking "Who else can I meet that would love to contribute to the future I would love to create?" It is amazing who the Universe brings to me that adds a totally new dimension to what I

STOP WAITING, START CREATING

am creating. If you didn't believe in competition, only in contribution and collaboration, what would be possible?

I asked my horse whispering friend if I could sit in the paddocks with her horses and write about what I discovered in my lessons with the horses. It came about because when she asks me for words to describe what occurred in the lesson, there is just energy, no words. When I sit in the paddock and have the space to receive, the words come. When I asked her this she also asked me 'would you like to play with music and horses? Oh yes, I would!!! I had not thought of that, even though watching a horse dance was where this adventure started years ago!! This is collaboration, contribution and co-creation all rolled into one. Where can it lead? Everywhere!!

When you undertake these kinds of adventures and experiments, you have to be willing for what shows up to be totally out of your control. You need to be ready for unexpected growth (in all senses of the word!). You have to know that whatever shows up is leading you to exactly where you are asking to go! Get ready. These energies exponentialise what is possible!

There are other ways to co-create and collaborate too. I love what performer Amanda Palmer has created with her Patreon offers. There are also many crowd-funding and crowd-sourcing platforms that allow you to create with people you've never met. Meet Kickstarter, GoFundMe, IndieGoGo and Kiva. They all offer different approaches to crowd-funding. Whatever you choose, start building your audience platform as soon as you can. It will help those magical connections show up.

It's time to give up being an island that creates alone. Even the best islands receive contribution from the ocean, the wind, the rain, the animals and birds and the sun!

Lisa Murray

Crowd-sourcing invites contribution from many other people. Over 2000 different crowd-sourcing platforms exist at the time of writing, fulfilling every need you can imagine! Check out 99Designs for your design needs, OpenIDEO and Change.Org for creating social change and CrowdCube for targeting investors. If you have an idea, somewhere online there is a crowd who can contribute to you!

THE HEDONISM OF FINISHING

Finishing. This may be the chapter you'd love to skip, but somehow you know if you could just get yourself to finish reading it, something will be different! Yes it will. For a start, you'll be able to tell the world you finished something!

Here's the thing, I love starting so much more than finishing. The result used to be hundreds or thousands of unfinished projects, half-cut ideas, scraps of possibilities and a big fat Guilt Monster who was waking me up day and night and pushing me ever harder into the arms of his friend Overwhelm Monster, who rarely shows up without Exhaustion Monster close behind.

Whenever the Monsters show up, I know that it's time for a project stocktake and some changes! I have a fast, simple Monster Removal process that clarifies which project to finish next. You can download your free Finishathon Starter Kit at www.CreativityLab.tv/Finish. That's where you start if the Monsters have already taken over your creation space. You'll get to see just how many unfinished projects you have pulling on your creative energies. AND you'll receive a simple system for making sense of it all and knowing what to let go of and what to finish next!

If the Monsters are only irregular visitors, you can take a different approach. Once I had the Monster Removalists in, I realised I had to put one simple rule in place.

Each month I finish at least one substantial project before I start any new projects.

Yes, I know it sounds ridiculously simple. It is. And it works! My reward for finishing well, fast and early is having the rest of the month to explore the new. To play with ideas, to have adventures, to collaborate and co-create and to discover unexpected talents. It's a lot more like living should be than the forceful 'nose to the grindstone until I die of exhaustion or starvation' method many people use to get projects finished.

One thing most of us don't ever ask is 'What is finished?' I've come to realise that finished is mostly that space where you draw a line in the sand and you say 'no more scope creep, this ships as is!' There is no obvious finish line for a book, a website, a painting or even a movie. It's finished when we say it is.

What would be possible if you moved the finish line forward rather than backwards? The tendency is to be always adding to the scope, so that finishing never becomes possible. What can you take away from the scope of the project that will allow you to finish faster and still offer your audience what they desire? In essence, what is the minimum viable product you can create? Use that as your finishing line. You can always upgrade or expand on it after you have launched and have some feedback on what your audience truly desires. Maybe they aren't asking for everything you'd like to offer!

It's finished when it is good enough to put into the world. Not perfect. Good enough. If you're reading this book there's a high chance your 'good enough' is way better than most people's. Truly! Trust me on this one!! What if you are way more amazing than you know?

If you are unsure, you can also ask your projects to tell you when they are finished and ready to go into the world. They know what is required to create greater possibilities, even if you are determined to keep feeding it long after the horse has bolted. I've discovered that even if I desire to give people 'the perfect product', it is often much more than they require. You have to know how to stop at the earliest moment of possibility, rather than at the 'I wish it was the end now' time, when you're totally done with the idea and cannot be bothered to finish!

The Adventure of Finishing

What is it that finishing is never anywhere near as thrilling as starting? You know what I'm talking about. Where the initial exhilaration of an amazing idea so quickly turns into the 'ho-hum' of just another thing on the to-do list...

We love the rush of over-stimulation that comes with the new. The energy that comes with curiosity, discovery and experimentation. The moment our creations become predictable, or we come too close to actually being successful, we back off, turning ourselves down and turning our projects off.

There is this moment in every project where you can make the choice to be bored and let your brilliant idea atrophy into nothing, or you can ask "Who or what can I add to this project that will expand it beyond my imagination?"

When we aren't in the conclusion of 'this is how I have to create this', we can make every iteration and forward movement exciting. Finishing once again becomes an adventure because you are constantly asking what you can create with your idea that you haven't considered before. You don't have to lose that thrilling start-up energy unless you choose! Here's what I know...

It's not your project that got boring... it was YOU! (Sorry!!)

Expansion doesn't have to mean more work. It can be adding people who will do the work you don't wish to do. It can be simplifying your creation so that it makes you more money for less work. It can be talking about the things no-one else talks about in ways that invite more people to your ideas.

When Seth Godin talks about shipping, he's talking about finishing. About putting your ideas into the world so others can enjoy them. There's hedonism in doing that. Hedonists are pleasure seekers. Imagine a world where you and your clients are always seeking pleasure... would you be bored with your ideas? Or would you be always asking what can you create that will up the pleasure quotient in the world?

STOP WAITING, START CREATING

Get the energy of the last project you finished…

◆ *Did you receive pleasure from making something that no-one else can?*

◆ *Did your creation give others pleasure?*

◆ *Did it open the doors to creating and generating more pleasure?*

◆ *Did it make the world more beautiful?*

◆ *Did finishing give you more energy and more space to create something new?*

When you don't finish, you are avoiding pain so that you cannot have pleasure. That is the weirdness of our 'logic'. It's why I suggest you give up logic in favour of pleasure! Hedonism isn't selfish. It's a creative, generative energy that invites the entire world to more!

Lisa Murray

Are Your Projects Shouting 'Finish ME!'?

There's this quiet whisper as you are going to sleep… 'the book… oh yes… the book… too tired now, maybe tomorrow.'

When you wake in the middle of the night wondering why 2am seems to be such a great time to wake up, there it is again. 'Remember me? I'm your book.' "Oh… yes… the book. I remember you…" and then you lay tossing and turning instead of getting up and writing just a few lines or sending that email off to your designer.

In the morning when you wake up there's something shouting at you. Oh! Surprise!!! It's your book! When you go on Facebook there are people talking about your topic… and you don't have anything to offer them. Yep… it's the book talking to you again.

Have you found yourself living in Groundhog Day with one special project? Are you using up ridiculous amounts of energy ignoring the project that could change your entire business or life… and maybe even the world?

It might not be a book for you, it might be a product, or a telecall series, or getting your tax done, or an artwork, or a proposal, or a relationship, or an adventure… we all have that 'one thing' - and if you're a prolific creator like I am, you may have hundreds or even thousands of unfinished 'one things'.

The whispers are talking to us non-stop because it's time - NOW - not in six months, or a year, or even next

STOP WAITING, START CREATING

lifetime. NOW! The world is asking for your gorgeous creation. Are you going to listen? Or are you going to keep telling yourself that it doesn't matter. That no-one wants what you've got. That there are already so many of them out there that your idea not being in the world won't make a difference. That you've gone this long without it, what's another lifetime or two?

Or maybe you pull out the big guns. You can't get it perfect. You're bored. You've got other more important ideas now. Good work! Do you notice how heavy these stories feel? What if none of this is true? What if you just love the thrill of starting more than the hedonism and adventure of finishing. And... what if finishing is just a choice? (And if this is you starting to make excuses again, may I refer you back to the 'What's Stopping You?' chapter in Section One?)

If you can't get finished for the pleasure of it, you could try a liberal application of bum glue — add it to the seat where you and your sweet body will get this thing finished and then sit there until you're done. I know, it sounds painful. But not finishing is even more painful. You know that quote from Wayne Dyer about dying with the music still in you? Does it ring any bells? And imagine the relief when the bum glue dries, your project doesn't have you pinned between a rock and a hard place anymore and you can peel your bum off the chair!!! Maybe you'll even get a bum-lift ;)

Sometimes we need help. Someone to talk to. A new strategy. A different approach. A collaborator or two. Some feedback. An injection of energy. Generative distractions instead of time-wasting distractors. Find a friend and have a Finishathon together - a day or three of crazy, mad, joyful finishing... how exhilarated will you be at the end?

How thrilled will your projects be? (Not to mention all the people who are SO bored of hearing you talk about your never-ending project. Sorry to those people who have been hearing about this book for way too long - I've been guilty of that one too!) And if you don't have a friend, join Business Alchemy Lab - there's a Finishathon every month!

There are other, much more fun alternatives to bum glue too... I'm sure your cute little butt is happy about that!! It doesn't like sharing you with all the other 'Buts'!! Have you noticed?

When your super special project is fully created... the world will be a better place, and you'll be able to have the joy of finishing! Maybe you'll even stop waking up at 2am!

Finishing doesn't have to mean an overdose of antidepressants with a side of wrist-slitting. It can be more non-stop champagne and chocolate cake... shall we play?

Stop Your Unfinished Projects From Distracting You

Unfinished projects are a distraction. They pull at you even after you've moved onto other things, dissipating your energy and leaving you with an attack of the Guilt Monster. "Why don't you love me anymore?' they cry, reminding you of other, happier days when they were your favourite child.

It doesn't have to be this way. You can stop that whiny sad little voice inside your head! Here are seven simple

STOP WAITING, START CREATING

ways to move your project forward. Sometimes forward doesn't look anything like we imagine!

1. *Stop rejecting your project and stop resisting finishing. Even if you don't work on it, if the project knows you still love it, it may be happy to wait! You can give it energy even if you don't actively do anything with it.*
2. *Turn it into something else - does it want to have idea babies with any of your other projects?*
3. *Make it bigger and more exciting - add people and resources. What could it be that you don't want to see?*
4. *Let it go. Throw it away. Let the idea fairy give it to someone else. Kiss it, stroke it, hug it and say 'thanks for the memories... good-bye!'*
5. *Gift your project to someone you know will love it more than you can. All ideas deserve good homes! You wouldn't treat your pet like this. Your project has its own life too! Who can bring it alive?*

6. Delegate the finishing bits to someone who loves that stuff or find a partner who would love to help you birth this baby. You don't have to do it all!
7. Just freaking FINISH the project! Yes... it can be that easy. If it was your love once, it can be again. You know the world is asking for your brilliance. What could show up if you would just give it fifteen minutes a day?

Finishing can be fun! Do you know that money follows joy? Would you make even more money if you finished a few things? (And they don't even have to be the same things that bring you money!! That's the magic of finishing!)

Ready to get finished? Your project will thank you! And you'll be able to say good-bye to the Guilt Monster. What magic could that create?

Making Finishing FUN!

Being productive definitely doesn't mean working non-stop until you fall apart. You'll finish more if you make your creative adventures playful and nurturing. Here are a few ideas to get started!

1. Invite your friends to play. Having a collective Finishathon is more fun than slaving away by yourself.

2. Find collaborators and co-creators to stimulate different and greater ideas.

3. Ask for contribution - fresh eyes create new possibilities.

4. Create in a different space. What inspiration can you receive?

5. Indulge in your vices. What if that's not wrong? Wine with writing is perfectly acceptable in my world.

6. Walk (or run). Repetitive physical motion gives your brain a rest from thinking.

7. Make your workspace playful. Add toys to your desk and colour to your creative space.

8. Keep your love notes and gratitude notes visible. (And write them for others!)

9. Know what (or who) makes you laugh and ask for laughter to show up every day.

10. Call or chat instead of emailing. Connection leads to more brilliant ideas.

11. Professional does not equal serious. Professional equals delivering something amazing. Stop confusing the two!

12. Have delicious food available (that doesn't take you hours to prepare). Or go hangout in a favourite cafe. It's my hedonistic way of creating.

13. Create outside. Nature is an amazing contribution. And micro-nature breaks offer aha moments!

14. Add plants or flowers to your environment - fresh air and beauty create more.

15. Take a nap.

16. Have play breaks where you get to be creative in a different way to your main project of the moment.

17. Take photos of your progress. Post them wherever you'll receive encouragement.

18. Make your creation time rewarding. For me, setting time to go play with horses is a huge motivator. What is it for you?

19. Create for the pleasure of creating, not only for the joy of finishing!

20. Have friends who you can have a quick chat with when you need a break. A quick conversation online can spark your ideas into new spaces.

21. Celebrate your milestones. Each chapter finished creates a book. Each graphic created makes a social media campaign. Each piece of art completed creates an exhibition.

22. Get a cleaner. What magic would you create if you didn't have to be distracted by mundane things?

23. Have hourly dance breaks. Or yoga stretches. Or dog-cuddles. Or sexy-time. Anything that moves your body into a different space and invites you to enjoy your creation time more.

24. Offer yourself a daily 'happiness review'. What could you add to this project to make it happy-making for you?

25. Create your ideas supersonically fast. Slow equals boredom for many people!

26. Make magic with something that has no specific outcome. Allow yourself to be led into new spaces by the energy of possibilities.

27. Immerse yourself in water - a bath, a pool, a float-tank, the ocean... our bodies are made of water and when you play in water, space is created and magic happens!

28. Read. Or listen to a podcast. So many times I am looking for a specific word and the person or page delivers

it right to me! What if contribution can come from everywhere? I've even had street signs give me the information I was seeking!!

29. Have a sketchbook or colouring-in book around for those moments when your hands need to move and your brain needs to rest. (I am a great watercolourist while on the phone!)

30. Have a list of videos or courses that you will watch when you have a spare moment. Indulge in that instead of Netflix! Or use Netflix as the inspiration for making your content way more fun for people!

This list is just the start. Make your own list! What is fun for you? What is indulgent? What is hedonistic? What is playful? What is magic? What is generative? What is energising? What is funny? What is blissful? What creates ease? What makes you sparkle? What is nurturing? What is different from every other person you know?

The only time finishing is not fun is when we turn it into the necessity of work! Wanna play?

STOP WAITING, START CREATING

What If Finishing Doesn't Have a Happy Ending?

You did it. You finally finished your masterpiece. And then the thing you feared most happened. You lost your work. Maybe the cat vomited on it. Maybe your computer lost the plot. Maybe no-one but you loved it. Maybe it didn't turn out as wonderfully as you imagined it could.

Here's what you do. Take a few deep breaths. Cry for a minute or ten if you need to. Then go play. Do something else. Allow the frustration in your body to dissipate. And then don't try to recreate, ask to out-create the brilliance you just were. Because you were brilliant, even if the world didn't recognise it yet.

Recognition is not everything - and for some people it stops them creating! You have to be willing to create whether anyone recognises your brilliance or not. Think Tesla, Da Vinci... there have been so many artists and creators who only got recognition after they died. You don't have to be one of them. And you won't be if you keep creating. The world is different now. We have the Internet.

What if the lost version of your idea was just the warm-up for something much greater? It's the same when the muse only visits for a fleeting moment and you lose the inspiration. You have to let it go. When you are willing to lose, you get to choose to create something even greater! Be willing to know there is so much more available. Sometimes I've invited someone different to play with me.

Lisa Murray

Or I've realised I wasn't that interested in the project anyway. There are many ways to get over the disappointment. Don't make it meaningful. Don't look for signs! Just ask... what else is possible beyond this?

You are infinite and so are your ideas. This was just one. If you don't get caught up in the significance of making time important, you'll know that something even more phenomenal is possible.

We've all been there. Don't make it serious. Don't create trauma and drama. Don't make it life or death. Move on. Your future is waiting for you. Living in the past will keep you there. Your life will love you for moving forward faster! Your business will adore you too. It's fun doing business with people who have ease... have you noticed?

~SECTION 4~
CREATING BEYOND WHAT EXISTS!

WHAT KIND OF WORLD WOULD YOU CREATE?

Controversy, Rebellion & Leadership

Creators who make a difference are both controversial and talented. They aren't satisfied with the status quo. They are willing to lead without followers. They are willing to be so different that people notice them, for no obvious reason! You know that energy of 'Is that person famous?' that you sometimes get walking down the street. It's that. A mystique. An energy and a presence that makes you different, even when you're pretending to be incognito. Nice try!

Are you truly invisible? Or are you bluffing and misleading the world as to your true brilliance and power? I'm just asking… What if you are way more phenomenal than you've ever allowed yourself to acknowledge? You don't have to believe it, you just need to recognise who you are. There is no other you. No-one else can create what you can. No-one else can be what you be. No-one else can invite people to a different possibility in exactly the way you can. You. Are. Brilliant. Whether you know it or not. If you are willing to know it, you can create beyond what exists.

You don't have to be well-known to have this kind of 'famous but not' intrigue. And you don't have to be a busy, loud extrovert either (and please don't shut yourself down if that is what you are…be you!).

However you express it in the world, you do have to be willing to be 1000000% YOU! Without apology, without shrinking, without pretending that you have nothing to offer, without making your ideas so small they are like a mosquito bite on the ass of the world. Persistent, annoying, slightly itchy, but not exactly changing anything in a big way. Is that you? Or are you so much greater than that?

Would you be willing to turn up your presence in every way and everywhere that you are different? Rather than turn yourself down so low that you have disappeared into the nothing that is everything?

What could you put into the world that would be controversial? It's not that difficult to be controversial. You just need to find your zone of genius and talk about the things that no-one else is talking about. Whatever points of view you have that go against the norm are the place to start. And when you start talking to people without editing yourself first, you're going to be surprised about what is 'controversial'. Let me tell you… it doesn't take much! People love fitting into the minimum viable options for living, way more than they love being the disruptor of realities they truly are.

STOP WAITING, START CREATING

It is still surprising to me that loving your work is controversial in some circles. You would not believe how many people think it is impossible to do work you love. Someone I know asked me 'what would you really love to do?' and I responded with 'write fiction books and live luxuriously off the proceeds'. To me this is totally doable. To them it was an unrealistic fantasy. We had to agree to disagree… I was not giving up my dream. And they were not giving up their 'that's impossible' point of view.

It's not even something I need to believe. I have a clear knowing that I can create this… when the timing is right. And there's no force in it… just flow! In the meantime, I write fiction on scraps of paper, in random moments when I finally give my senses enough space to wonder and wander. There's not a story yet, but there are some beautiful words. This is how you invite your biggest dreams into fruition. I promise you.

Rebellion Is Not The Answer

Being different and creating controversy is not about rebellion. That's an old energy that has no place. We don't need to rebel to create, we just need to be ALL that we are. It IS possible to create a different reality from the energy of harmony and without making yourself less. You are a visionary - when you BE it, you create change at the other end of the Universe.

At most of my corporate jobs I was the unconventional one. The one who mostly wouldn't go to meetings unless there was a really big carrot. (Never saw one of those!) The one who said what I thought, even if it wasn't politically correct. The one who would take a chance on someone, based on an awareness, rather than what they looked like on paper. The one who, at the age of 21, in my first 'marketing manager' role, called up the state marketing manager and refused to implement the marketing plan because it was shite. (Yes... I got to write my own plan and that was fun for a moment.)

As I got older, I was the one finding ways to make my workplaces kinder and more fun for the people in them, because I was confused about why we had to suffer at work. Who says working can't be the most creative, generative, engaging and empowered space we have?

I've always been the one pushing the boundaries. One of the things that has surprised me most in life was the discovery that not everyone wants more. Not everyone is asking for something greater. How did I discover this world-breaking news? Let's just say not everyone saw my unconventional choices as a contribution.

Some people saw it as bad that I didn't follow the rules or do what I was told. Bad that I got pay increases just because I asked, and they didn't. Bad that I didn't do what it took to 'fit in' with their limitations. Bad that I enjoyed change. Bad that I wanted to create something that hadn't existed before. Bad that I saw deadlines as more than a little bit flexible. Bad that I would question their decisions. Bad that I supported the other unorthodox people in my area. Bad that I didn't 'do things how we do them around here.'

Bad that I would go to lunch with my other 'bad' friends and not come back because I'd had a few drinks. The powers that were never worked it out that I would have had to not so politely let them know about their

STOP WAITING, START CREATING

incessant stupidity if I didn't go to lunch. It was my way of letting off steam and defragging the intensity of awareness I lived with. Personally I'd say they got off lightly!! I have heard it was not so much fun to be on the end of the kind of tough love I used to offer, without any regard to who you were. I have given more than one CEO the presence of my mind! Not to be mean, but to make them aware that change was required. Some listened, some offered lip service and some decided they had all the answers. I'm grateful for every one of them. You allowed me to know who I am, with or without your approval.

People made it 'bad' that my ideas were different. Bad that I thought planning was for the birds 'What do you mean you don't have a ten year plan?' ... umm no I don't need one, I'm way more aware than that!! When I look back, my list of 'bads' could go on forever. And it is exactly that list that makes my life worth living. Truly!

What is funniest about all of this is that I never saw myself as a rebel. In my head I was always trying to fit-in. Always trying to make it perfect for everyone. Except that I just couldn't. No matter how hard I tried. I could never get 'the rules' right. And I used to make myself so wrong for this. As Access Consciousness founder Gary Douglas describes it, my wrongness was my strongness. I would have bored myself to death (literally!!) if I had fitted in the way people wanted me to.

My 'rebellion' wasn't born out of being difficult. It was born out of trusting my knowing. Trusting that I knew something that others didn't. Even when all the evidence pointed in the other direction. Sometimes it paid off. Sometimes those above me didn't appreciate my awareness (or my willingness to mention the elephant in the room) and they set me free to pursue a different approach. Either way, I got to have more adventures. I've never left a job that I loved more than the paycheck. (Okay, except for maybe one... and it too would have got boring within a few months!)

If the money is the only thing keeping you where you are, it might be time to create a different possibility. And you don't have to destroy what you've got before you create an alternative. You just need to ask some questions about what you would truly LOVE to create. The possibility is there... you create the path by taking the first half-step!

Is rebellion going to create the future you would love to create? Or is it a resistance and reaction to what was that is already on its way out? Rebellion is an old energy that rarely generates something greater. Often when we rebel, we are using our considerable creative capacities against ourselves. We are making our life into a series of 'for and against' choices that bear no relevance to what we truly desire to choose. There is no allowing in resistance. No flow. No exploration of ideas or creativity. No ease. No spontaneity. No flexibility. There is only limitation.

Being different is not about proving how different you are. It is not about dyeing your hair orange with green dots to show the world you are different. Or wearing ugly clothes so you can stand out. It is not about swearing to be cool. (And I'm not being prudish here - I love swearing for the energy it releases!) It is not about making everything 'normal' wrong. That is all called rebellion. It's the weakest way of being different. Why? Because you aren't creating a greater reality. You are simply showing your judgements of what is.

When I was being 'bad' at work, most of the time I was creating something greater. (Except when I was just

STOP WAITING, START CREATING

trying to be annoying because I was frustrated by the stupidity around me). In being me, even when it 'cost me' by this realities standards, I was asking to create something that would allow people to be more of who they are. Something that would offer more choice and more possibilities, instead of it being all about the blind leading the blind into ever darker and narrower alleyways of dead-ends and limitation. You have to know what you are choosing. Don't make yourself wrong. Just choose what will create more from this moment forward.

True 'rebellion' is about taking the real you out of hiding. Not splashing yourself about like a page three 'model' desperate for your next gig, but being who you truly are. With no apologies and no limits. Most of the people I know who are really really different rarely talk about it - they are being it every second of the day. Talk is cheap. Hair-dye is cheap. Pretending to be different while settling for an alternate set of limitations that is just not quite as common as the mainstream set of limitations is cheap... and nasty!

Why nasty? The person you most rip-off is you. Are you willing to settle for that? Are you willing to treat you as worth less? Or are you getting the vibe that creating is all about BEing everything you are? The world is waiting for you. Is now YOUR time?

Lisa Murray

Your World...

"Had I not created my whole world, I would certainly have died in other people's."
~ **Anais Nin**

How much do you love the movies where a totally different world is created? Avatar? The Matrix? Harry Potter? Tomorrowland? What's cool about being a brilliant creator is we don't need to wait for a movie to start creating the world we would love to live in.

We have the capacities, talent and ability to create a very different world from where we are. Have you ever considered that we live on one of the most spectacular planets in existence? The only time we don't have magic is when we refuse it. Magic exists in every moment we allow it to.

Here's a simple place to start. Think of the last five things you complained about. Have you ever been or done that? What would be different if you never did that again? What could you do or be or create instead? What is the magic you would LOVE to bring to the world that would out-create each of these situations? If you stopped telling yourself you 'can't' or that what you desire is 'impossible', what doors could that open? What would you need to be or do or choose that could change everything in a second?

The funny thing is, when I ask people these kinds of questions in coaching sessions, they tend to look at me like bunnies frozen in headlights. Like 'WHAT? What do you

STOP WAITING, START CREATING

mean I can change this?' Yes... you can. Or you wouldn't be reading this book. There are so many ways of creating change that go beyond activism and fighting.

Here's another way you can begin to create the change you would love to see in the world. This is one of my favourite activities for Creativity Lab live event participants. And it's a great way for starting to get a sense of the directions you would like your life to move towards. If you are stuck in "I don't know what my purpose is. Poor me. I can't start until I know." This is the exploration for you! Hint: there is no one right answer! What if there are literally a thousand ideas just waiting for you to say YES! Let's play...

Imagine the world 1000 years in the future. Imagine it is a world YOU have created. What would be different?

◆ *How would people create?*

◆ *How would people be with each other?*

◆ *How would we treat the earth?*

◆ *What would work be like?*

◆ *Would there still be money or would we have a system that creates greater possibilities?*

◆ *What would no longer exist?*

◆ *What have we not yet imagined that would be totally normal?*

You can play with these questions from the energy of what would be different, or you can explore the tangible realities. Dream bigger than you have ever have. Explore. Expand your vision. Have you ever acknowledged how much change there has been in the last thousand years? What else could be possible if we use what we know now as a launching pad into a future not yet imagined?

Once you have a sense of the world you would love to live in, start creating it by asking:

◆ *'What energies can I add to my life NOW that would create this for the future?"*

◆ *'What choices can I make today that will create this future faster?'*

◆ *'What can I be or do different that will allow this future to show up now?'*

When I last visited Oslo, there were Tesla electric cars everywhere. They are beautiful! When Tesla was inventing for the future, he didn't stop just because no-one was interested his ideas. And just recently, the Tesla Foundation released the patents on all Tesla inventions so that the world can play. Talk about creating a different future!!

When you create for the pleasure of it, rather than the money, you create a future that future generations will thank you for. And what if you would be willing to have the money too? How much fun would that be?

STOP WAITING, START CREATING

What would you like to create that you think is impossible? Yes… start there. Because once you make the choice to start, you dive into a wonderland that is greater than anything Alice had access to. For a start, you don't have to make yourself smaller. You can BE more and more will show up.

Your creative energy is available every day! Whatever you create, there's always the choice to create more. If you become super successful you can rest on your laurels and still be performing the same old circus tricks at 80, or you can continually out-create yourself. The most fun 'old' people I know are still creating.

I learned to ride a horse from a 93 year old man. It was an incredible pleasure as he always showed me what I could do, rather than what I couldn't. I'm truly grateful for that gift. It has taken me far beyond what I expected. What have you told yourself you can't create that you actually can? Go create it!

~SECTION 5~
WHAT'S NEXT?

CONNECT WITH LISA MURRAY & CREATIVITY LAB

Lisa Murray is the Australian founder of Creativity Lab, a thriving international business which invites you to Nurture Your Ideas Into Life™. MBA qualified, Lisa is an unconventional business coach, prolific writer and creative adventurer. 'Stop Waiting, Start Creating' is her first book. Lisa offers innovative online programs and live events for entrepreneurs, change agents and creatives who are willing to go beyond the status quo.

Creativity Lab brings people together to create and generate new possibilities for the future. It's an experimental and co-creative lab full of world-changers, future-creators and difference-makers.

Find out more at www.CreativityLab.tv

Lisa Murray

Creativity Lab – Online Programs

If you are ready for a different way of creating your ideas in business, become a member of Business Alchemy Lab. It's an intuitive approach to creating your work that allows for flexibility, ease, flow, spontaneity and magic!

Join us at www.BusinessAlchemyLab.com or check out the free video tips on the Youtube playlist!

If you are tired of forcing yourself to meet your goals, hustling, pushing to make things happen, and kicking your own ass (not to mention the sight of your to-do list is giving you burnout!) join the Nurture Projects. What if nurturing your life, your ideas and creative projects into the world could allow them to become far greater, in ways you haven't yet imagined?

www.CreativityLab.tv/Nurture

Creativity Lab – Live Events

Creativity Lab events are held all over the world. These events are often 'hands-on' and a great way to move forward with your projects with Lisa's personal contribution.

More at www.CreativityLab.tv/Events

STOP WAITING, START CREATING

Private Coaching With Lisa Murray

Lisa offers a limited number of private coaching spots each month where you can dive deep into what is stopping you and change it! She also offers business coaching and mentoring for entrepreneurs and business owners seeking a different way forward.

For more information or to book a session see www.CreativityLab.tv/Breakthrough

Connect With Lisa Online

FREE RESOURCES

The Adventurous Creator Podcast:
http://bit.ly/LisaPodcast

YouTube:
https://www.youtube.com/user/LisaMurray990

Soundcloud:
http://www.soundcloud.com/creativitylab

SOCIAL MEDIA

Creativity Lab Facebook Group:
https://www.facebook.com/groups/668531593196420/

Creativity Lab Facebook Page:
https://www.facebook.com/CreativityLabLIVE/

Instagram:
https://www.instagram.com/creativitylab/

Pinterest:
https://au.pinterest.com/lisamurray/

Twitter:
https://twitter.com/CreativeThrival

Google+:
https://plus.google.com/u/0/+LisaMurray990

LinkedIn:
https://www.linkedin.com/in/enrichedenterprises

Huffington Post Blogger –
http://www.huffingtonpost.com/lisa-murray/

REFERENCES

Research[1]
2 hr break - http://www.fastcompany.com/3049122/hit-the-ground-running/the-scientific-case-for-taking-a-two-hour-lunch-break

Law of Jante[2]
http://en.wikipedia.org/wiki/Law_of_Jante

www.ingramcontent.com/pod-product-compliance
Lightning Source LLC
Chambersburg PA
CBHW071944110426
42744CB00030B/280